**WANT TO LEARN THE SECRETS THAT HAVE
HELPED OLYMPIC ATHLETES WIN GOLD
MEDALS . . . ACTORS WIN ACADEMY
AWARDS . . . LAW STUDENTS PASS THE BAR
EXAM?
OF COURSE YOU DO!**

Imagine being able to harness a power beyond the capability of the most powerful computer. Imagine possessing a confidence so strong and deeply rooted nothing can shake it. Imagine taking an exam in your hardest subject and getting an A. Imagine raising your athletic ability far beyond your present level. Imagine increasing your popularity with friends and smoothing your relationships with family. Imagine improving your SAT scores by 100 points. Imagine being the person who always gets the ''lucky breaks'' . . . stays healthy . . . remains cool under pressure—and more!

**MATT OECHSLI WILL HELP YOU DEVELOP THE
POWERFUL MENTAL TECHNIQUES AND
ACTION PLAN TO MAKE YOUR DREAMS A
REALITY IN . . .**

MIND POWER FOR STUDENTS

THE ULTIMATE IN ''COOL''

MIND POWER

FOR STUDENTS

MATT OECHSLI

St. Martin's Paperbacks

All client names have been changed to guarantee their confidentiality.

MIND POWER FOR STUDENTS

Copyright © 1996 by Matt Oechsli.

ISBN: 0-312-96042-5

Printed in the United States of America

St. Martin's Paperbacks edition/October 1996

10 9 8 7 6 5 4 3 2

Contents

Introduction

"The quality of a person's life is in direct proportion to their commitment to excellence, regardless of their chosen field of endeavor."
—Vincent T. Lombardi

What to Expect from Using This Book

Top athletes freely admit that 75 to 90 percent of their success is due to mastering the mental side of sports. In fact, many top athletes regularly engage in mental training programs. Jack Nicklaus describes the visualization aspect of his mental training in his book, *Golf My Way*: "First I 'see' the ball where I want it to finish, nice and white and sitting up high on the bright green grass. The scene quickly changes, and I 'see' the ball going there: its path, trajectory, and shape, even its behavior landing. Then there is sort of a fade-out, and the next scene shows me making the kind of swing that will turn the previous images into reality."

Well before Nicklaus took golf by storm, two historic sporting events brought the powers of the mind to the attention of the world. The first happened back in ancient history—1954—and involved running the mile. Prior to May 6 of that year, no one had ever run a mile in less than four minutes. Although many tried—the Greeks used wild animals to chase the runners in hopes that they would run faster—some came close, but none succeeded in breaking this four-minute barrier. This caused many experts to believe the barrier was physiological—that human bodies weren't designed to run that fast.

What was even more astonishing than Roger Bannister's historic run that broke the four-minute mile in 1954 was the number of runners who broke the four-minute mile immediately afterwards. As Bannister recalled, "Everyone used to think it was quite impossible, and beyond the reach of any runner." Human physiology didn't change, but the self-limiting belief that a four-minute mile was impossible to break was shattered. Such was mind power at work.

The other historic event involved a Russian weightlifter, Vasily Alexeev. In 1970 he lifted 501 pounds over his head. Prior to this lift, it was argued that it was a physiological impossibility to lift 500 pounds over one's head. Soon after, many other weightlifters duplicated Alexeev's feat. Why? Mind power.

As Arnold Schwarzenegger said, referring to this feat of strength, "They believed it was possible. The body didn't change. How could the body change that much? It was the same body. But the mind was different. Mentally it's possible to break records. Once you understand that, you can do it."

In the 1984 Olympics, gymnast Mary Lou Retton mentally rehearsed every move before winning the gold. Greg Louganis, the world's greatest diver, was known to visualize each dive, in precise detail, forty times before climbing the platform. And the beat goes on.

Mind power goes far beyond the glamour of sports. It impacts every aspect of our lives. Imagine being able to visualize your score on a test and then get it. Or making that winning move on the playing field and then winning. How about seeing yourself asking the girl of your dreams for a date and getting it? Nicklaus became one of golf's biggest winners through applying "Mind Power" to his golf talent. Arnold Schwarzenegger used it to become the world's most successful bodybuilder. You too can have access to this vital source of energy. If you can daydream you can master this awesome power and get almost anything you want. In fact, this is just the tip of the iceberg. Mastering the powers of your mind can accomplish this and more. All you need is imagination.

You are about to learn how to use your mind to get what you want out of life. Just as most top athletes currently use some form of mental training to get more out of their athletic talents, I know in the near future most students will be applying similar mental training to every important aspect of life. The world is too competitive to do otherwise. You are about to get a head start.

The chapters that follow are specifically designed to take you through each stage of the Mind Power process that I teach in six sessions over a 120-day period. You will find the entire focus centered around mental training that deals with personal growth. Academics, athletics, family, career . . . in other words, *Mind Power for Students* will touch your entire life.

I have been teaching Mind Power techniques for the past 15 years. During this time I have witnessed many success stories. Unfortunately, I have seen some capable people fail. The Mind Power success stories all had one important factor in common—they were committed to winning the game of life and had mastered the powers of mind.

You can be your own success story. By simply following the techniques, principles, and exercises exactly as they are presented in *Mind Power for Students*, you will:

- Unlock your true potential
- Increase your grades
- Study better—in less time
- Boost your confidence
- Increase your self-esteem
- Break your bad habits
- Develop good personal habits

- Improve your athletic ability
- Master the art of Role Model Power
- Make your own self-programming cassette tape
- Master the powers of your mind
- Improve family relationships
- Gain control of your life
- Improve your relationships at home

As evidenced by this lengthy but partial list of Mind Power benefits, every success in life, big or small, originates from within. Napoleon created battle plans from daydreams in a sandbox. Albert Einstein was an uneducated 16-year-old when he imagined himself riding on a beam of light as it traveled through space at 186,000 miles per second. An infant imagines himself walking long before he takes that first step. Michael Jordan imagined winning each of his NBA championships.

Successful people train their mind to the extent that they know where they're going in life. Through mental training you will be able to experience similar control over your life. You will be able to clearly visualize your successes long before they happen. Like all achievers, you will see yourself winning and enjoying all the benefits that come with life's successes.

Goal-focused visualization is the internal program of a winner. It's the mental pictures that help create an unshakable self-expectancy. You know you will succeed far in advance of your accomplishments. It is this visualization, these internal tapes, that continually refuel your confidence and achievement drive. These tapes you have programmed in your mind will provide the strength necessary to keep moving forward in the midst of adversity. Mind Power, through mental training, will teach you to act from strength, consistently, day after day.

Are you ready to tap into this awesome power? Keep reading as you start on a journey that will give you control of your destiny.

Chapter 1

Rules of Mind Power

"Chance favors the prepared mind."
—Louis Pasteur

Your mental powers go far beyond the classroom and the athletic field. "I can't take it anymore! My mother wants me to be perfect and she's driving me crazy. What can I do?" moaned 15-year-old Janice Hall, as she sat dejectedly in my office.

"I get one C on my report card and I'm lectured about not studying enough. I'm one of at least twenty-five who don't make the soccer team and my mother tells me it's because I'm too fat. I know she wants only the best for me, but doesn't she understand that I'm trying? It's gotten to the point where my confidence is shot. All I think about is no matter what I do I can't meet my mother's expectations."

As with many frustrated teenagers, Janice wanted someone to listen and attempt to understand her plight. As I listened she became more confident in expressing her feelings. And when I told her that what was she was experiencing, unfortunately, was not unusual in today's world, she was visibly relieved. I explained how it had become rather commonplace for well-meaning parents to put too much pressure on their children, and that the results were rarely positive and the parents were often clueless.

Ironically, Janice was sitting in my office at her mother's request. She had flunked two courses, recently started smoking cigarettes, and was becoming defiant at home. What caused Janice to change from being a good student with a happy-go-lucky disposition to a teenager on the edge? Why was her mother finally getting on her nerves after all these years? Why was Janice allowing her mother to ruin her grades and her confidence? Maybe you can relate to Janice. Maybe you have a friend in a similar situation.

YOUR PERSONAL TAPES

You are who you are, today, because of the tapes that you have playing inside your head. Your accomplishments are what they are for the same reason—the tapes playing inside your head. Janice Hall's life was on a downward slide because of these tapes. Her mother, with the best of intentions spiced with sheer ignorance, was the reason her tapes had become destructive.

What is fascinating about our vast and powerful inner dimension, which I refer to as Mind Power, is that most people are aware it exists and need only a little guidance to understand how to use it constructively. After only a few minutes of talking, Janice realized what was happening to her and why.

I had insisted that Janice's mother not question her about our sessions and that she also back off in discussing school with her daughter. "I don't know if she is going to like the idea of not being involved," said Janice. "I think it's going to be easier for me to change and get control of my life than it will be for my mother. She actually believes that my homework would never get done if she wasn't constantly looking over my shoulder. This is going to be a big step for her. She's really set in her ways. All I have to do is ignore her and change that little voice in my head that's been telling me 'you can't please her.' ''

Janice's intuition was correct. She had just verbalized what was going to be her future. It would be easier for Janice to master the powers of her mind than her mother. The same holds true for any adult; parent, teacher, coach. . . . Like Janice, you are in your ''prime-time'' development years. It will be much easier for you to sink your teeth into the necessary mental training and change your tapes than it is for most adults.

All I mean is if both you and your parents were golfers, it would be easier for you to apply visualization techniques to your game. Because it's your prime-time development stage in life, you are less analytical and more open to suggestion. Right?

As for Janice, she took to heart the mental training you are about to learn and regained control of her life. Her mother never thought it necessary to go through the program, but at least she followed my basic ground rule for overbearing parents: Back Off! She stopped asking Janice about school, going over her homework, and questioning her friends. Thus Janice was able to rebuild her confidence by reprogramming her own internal tapes. The last time we talked she had quit smoking and was focused on college. Her mother, pleased with the results, was still at a loss for words—she didn't understand Mind Power.

I refer to these internal voices as tapes because they play automatically, and they play whatever is recorded. Just like a pre-recorded cassette tape you listen to in your Walkman, these tapes play whatever is recorded every time they are played. If you sense that your internal tapes are holding you back, you have two options: re-record the tapes, or stop listening to them.

STUDENTS BEWARE

Because you are in those prime-time development years, the internal tapes you now are developing are likely to be with you throughout your life. Many a promising future has been ruined during these years. Alas, most adults have the wrong recordings in their head. The messages they hear are too negative. So when parents and teachers are listening to tapes constantly playing negative messages like, "You can't do this. . . ." "You're not good enough." "What's the use?" they are transferring this destructive pattern of thinking to you. You are about to stop this unfortunate habit dead in its tracks.

Please understand there is no miraculous solution. But there are definite laws of nature. As it states so clearly in the Bible, "As a man thinketh in his heart, so is he." Mind Power and mental training is a natural process that will put you in control of such thinking.

YOUR ADVANTAGE

Everyone is looking for that competitive advantage, scheming to get ahead, win the game, get into that choice college, get the girl or boy of his or her dreams. Your first step in mastering Mind Power is to accept the fact that "the competition" is you. You have no outside competition! Your only competition is determined by the limits you set for yourself. The tendency of students is to constantly look over their shoulder at their peers, when they need to be focusing attention on their own mental training.

All winners understand that winning is an inside game. They realize that their own accomplishments define their self-esteem, discipline, and future. Mind Power is the ultimate tool that can be used for virtually anything, anywhere. Learning how to effectively use your Mind Power is like playing poker with a stacked deck of cards. It increases your odds in everything you do. Used properly, Mind Power is what makes people appear "lucky."

Would you like the odds stacked in your favor? Would you feel guilty if you went through life with your friends calling you "lucky," always seeming to have an advantage? As you begin your work in mastering Mind Power, consider the words written by Arnold Schwarzenegger in his autobiography *Arnold: The Education of a Body-builder* (Pocket Books, 1982): "The mind is a dynamo, a vital source of energy that can be negative and work against you—or you can harness it to give yourself unbelievable workouts and build the physique that lives up to your wildest expectations."

Think about that statement. How often have you gotten down on yourself because you felt you weren't living up to your wildest expectations? How many times have you asked yourself, "If I could only . . . ?"

- get lucky
- have more confidence in myself
- get better grades
- reach my athletic potential
- be more popular
- have a better relationship with my parents
- develop the discipline to break my bad habits
- have more insight into others
- make more out of my life
- have an advantage

Everyone expects more out of life, including students. Each person wants to better him- or herself, have more confidence, more ability, reach higher levels of achievement, live up to their wildest dreams. Whether it's in the classroom, the gym, or with friends, imagine functioning at a higher level. An exciting thought, isn't it? But few ever go for it. Imagine being able to harness a power beyond the capability of the most powerful computer. Imagine having a confidence so strong and deep-seated that nothing could shake it. Imagine succeeding where you previously struggled. In the classroom, you will get better grades. In sports, you will raise the level of your play. With friends, you will ooze self-assurance. Within your family, all of your relationships will be improved.

By learning how to harness this power of mind you will accomplish more than you can imagine. This is what *Mind Power for Students* is all about. In every chapter you will interact with proven Mind Power secrets that have helped students improve grades, build confidence and basically win in every arena they competed in. These are the same tools that have helped Olympic athletes win gold medals, accounting students pass the CPA exam, and law students pass the bar exam. There is no real secret. But yes, there is. . . .

The secret is learning how to use Mind Power constructively and consistently. Essentially, it's a discipline. If you're disciplined enough to brush your teeth and bathe, you've got what it takes to master everything in this book. You can consistently use your Mind Power constructively. Every exercise, every reference, and every chapter is geared toward accomplishing such discipline. I have seen students get A's where they'd been flunking, improve their SAT scores by as much as 200 points, quit using drugs, cure migraine headaches, lose weight, stop smoking, win tennis tournaments—even help parents and teachers by applying the techniques you are about to learn. Cool, isn't it?

Such COOL is the discipline of constructive mind power. All great athletes have their own methods for harnessing the constructive powers of the mind so they can live up to their wildest expectations. So they can live their dreams. Mental training, Mind Power—call it anything you want—does not discriminate. Consider it the ultimate equal-opportunity employer. Rest assured, it is available to you. Why? Because it is you.

It's about the personal power you possess. And it's about putting you in action. Mental training requires action. Why is one of your friends sad while another is happy? Why is one student popular and full of self-confidence and another is lonely and miserable? Why is it that some students score well on tests while others fail? Why do some athletes respond well under pressure while others become a bundle of nerves? Why are some people always sick while others never catch any germ that's going around?

The reason for such differences in people can usually be attributed to the application of Mind Power. When used destructively, nothing good ever happens. When used constructively, "luck" becomes your companion. You become the person who always gets the breaks. It's one of the fundamental laws of nature. You can be certain that people who aren't actively involved in training their mind to work constructively are at the mercy of destructive mind power.

YOUR CRYSTAL BALL

Get used to the idea of having your own crystal ball. You will be using it a lot as you get involved with mental training. For now I want you to think of what you would like to change as the result of applying yourself throughout this book. What would you like to improve? Grades, sports, confidence, family relationships, spiritual . . . whatever. Select four areas and simply write them on a blank piece of paper under the heading "Crystal Ball Exercise."

Actually, instead of a blank piece of paper, it's probably a good time to designate a notebook as your "Mind

Power Notebook.'' Get a clean notebook, as you will be doing a lot of Mind Power exercises in it.

Now pretend that you are holding a crystal ball in your hands that will enable you to look into and create your future. Okay, you're now looking into this crystal ball and seeing yourself living up to your wildest expectations, just as you would desire your life to be, in each of the four areas you've listed in your notebook. Don't worry about the details of how you're going to get there. Consider this just the beginning of reaching out for your wildest dreams. They are about to become your new image. These dreams are very likely to be realized from investing yourself in the upcoming mental training.

Essentially, you are beginning with the end in mind. Like a first-year medical student seeing herself as an emergency room physician before ever stepping into an emergency room. With this crystal ball you are seeing yourself getting exactly what you want—in advance. This is an essential aspect of Mind Power which you will learn about in much greater detail in subsequent chapters. For now, you are going to begin with the end in mind.

Beginning with the end in mind automatically gets you using your mind constructively. It becomes your virtual reality. So let's get into training. Do you feel like getting lucky? Sure you do. Hey, you already are.

There are so many simple tools to help you master Mind Power. Consider role models, for example. There has been little or no emphasis placed on role models in schools. Yet any student of human behavior will agree that personal development is tremendously enhanced by a positive human example. The most rapid growth in children occurs when they still identify parents as role models. This is why your parents, and now possibly your teachers, have played such a pivotal role in creating your personal tapes. Not all parents and teachers are positive role models—but, of course, you're well aware of this.

Are you using your mind constructively? Are you in

control of your internal tapes? Do you have a positive role model? Keep on reading if you are interested in learning how to control your internal tapes. Once you know how to do it, it's quite easy. So read on, get involved with all the exercises, and above all—GET LUCKY!

WRAP-UP

- Your personal, internal tapes control your life.
- Parents often mean well but create destructive pressure that has a negative impact on your personal tapes.
- You can reprogram your tapes—remember Janice.
- You are in your prime-time development years.
- If you can daydream, you can master Mind Power.
- Your crystal ball will help you begin with the end in mind.
- It's your time—Get lucky!

Chapter 2

Controlling Your Internal Tapes

"There is nothing either good or bad, but thinking makes it so."

—William Shakespeare

No one personality is better suited for mastering Mind Power than another. Take baseball's two greatest home-run hitters: the colorful and volatile Babe Ruth, and the quiet and even-tempered Hank Aaron. Though both had different personalities and temperaments, each possessed absolute control over his thoughts as they related to hitting a baseball.

As behavioral researcher and author Dr. Shad Helmstetter writes in his book *The Self-Talk Solution*: "One of the most important discoveries in recent years has been the role of what our own casual thinking plays in the shaping of our lives." Experts used to regard thoughts as harmless, abstract, fleeting bits of consciousness that everyone had and little could be done about them. How wrong they were.

Opinion has come full circle, as neuroscientists have discovered that thoughts are actually electrical impulses which trigger both electrical and chemical reactions in the brain. Far from being abstract bits of fleeting consciousness, your thoughts impact the chemical activity in your brain. In effect, they are electrochemical triggers. Dr.

Helmstetter is right, you need to begin paying close attention to your thoughts as they relate to life.

Good or bad, it makes no difference to your brain. Good thoughts trigger a positive chemical reaction, bad thoughts create a negative reaction. Which is why your mind seems to flow with creativity, your body becomes fully energized, and a "can-do" spirit dominates your every action—when you're happy about something. Conversely, anger is the perfect stumbling block to happiness; it's almost as if your brain released a toxic substance into your nervous system that triggers more destructive thoughts and behaviors.

I want you to think of your thoughts as internal tapes playing inside your head. A little computer jargon will help make this association and help paint a picture of how your internal tapes are programmed.

GARBAGE IN/GARBAGE OUT

Negative programming versus positive programming is the issue here. Garbage in/garbage out—this oft-used phrase from computer technology—provides a good working example of how the mind is programmed. You can get a fairly good feel for the difference between negative and positive programming through the following examples. As you will discover, it's a very subtle process.

Garbage In (Misinformation)	Garbage Out (Behavior)
1. "I'm no good at tests."	1. Test choking—poor test results.
2. "I'm not ever good enough."	2. Failure to really give your best effort.
3. (Write your own)	3. (Write your own)

None of this is new news. An ancient Silesian proverb proves the timelessness of this message: "No one deceives us more than our own thoughts." It's hard to imagine Babe Ruth saying to himself, "I'll never get another home run."

Crystal Ball (Goal-Oriented) Thoughts

Positive Input	Positive Output (Behavior)
1. "I love the challenge of tests."	1. Consistently higher test scores.
2. "I always give my best effort."	2. Consistent accomplishments and growth.
3. (Write your own.)	3. (Write your own.)

As I'm sure you're already aware, and the garbage-in/garbage-out exercise simply reminded you, repeating negative thoughts poisons your internal tapes. It can damage your confidence, ruin your grades, and kill all your natural enthusiasm. It has been my experience that far too many students are victims of such destructive programming. And, many are totally unaware of this. Cynical students waste a lot of time trying to convince themselves that they're "cool"—but it's really just a cover-up. They don't know real COOL. Mind Power is what real COOL is all about. Nothing more or less.

So now I am going to share with you the ultimate in COOL. You are about to learn how to reprogram your internal tapes and begin taking control of that awesome power of mind every human being possesses.

PUBLIC BAD HABIT NUMBER 1

According to Dr. Helmstetter, 75 percent or more of our early programming was most likely negative—which, if one applies the basic law of cause and effect, automatically leads to developing the habit of negative self-talk; which, in turn, becomes our internal programming. Since very few people, including most adults, are not taught how to use their conscious thoughts to counteract this natural occurrence, most people do exactly the opposite: They abuse themselves by thinking too much.

Because so much of our early programming is negative, it's natural that too much thinking translates into too much negative thinking. Think of the last time you thought, "I hate tests!" There's probably a good chance you scored below your ability on that test. Why? Not because of that single thought, but rather because that single thought was repeated, over and over, in your subconscious mind. Through such repetition it had been recorded onto your internal tapes without you even being aware. So naturally you had trouble concentrating when you tried to study. It's hard to do anything well if we hate doing it.

So remember a simple rule of the mind: too much thinking leads to negative thinking. As you overplayed your thoughts about an upcoming test, doubt crept in and you became acutely aware of all the reasons you might do poorly. You replayed all the negativity associated with test-taking. You started worrying. Not only did you worry about this particular test, you worried about your other classes, you worried about getting into the college of your choice, about letting your parents down, you worried. . . .

Whether you followed my above-given scenario of worry or had your own version, the fact is that negative thoughts lead to worry. Anytime you find yourself worrying about something, you are actually killing any type of productive behavior. Think of worry as a cancer to productive behavior. It's the ultimate in destructive mind power.

NEGATIVE PROGRAMMING

This is true in every aspect of life. I recall a successful businessman who came to me for help in overcoming his fear of speaking in public. This literally petrified him, and it did so to such an extent that he recently passed up a lucrative promotion because he was afraid he would be asked to speak frequently. And this is what prompted his visit to my office.

His thoughts were so negative that he couldn't sleep for nights prior to any event where he would be required to speak. He worried about appearing foolish, sounding boring, and delivering a message nobody cared about hearing. Guess what usually happened when he spoke? You got it. His worries become reality. He choked up, looked foolish, and people had trouble paying attention to what he was saying because they were feeling sorry for him.

All of this is now history. The executive learned how to recognize the negative thoughts that caused his worry. Once he recognized this thought pattern, which I call the "negative programming cycle," he was able to use some of the tools you're about to learn and he changed it. He learned how to control the pattern of his thoughts. Within a week he had given two speeches and joined a local toastmasters club (an organization to help people speak in public).

This man's story highlights what is so amazing about Mind Power. Actually, it's what makes Mind Power so exciting. Within one week the executive was able to experience significant change. He got results. Properly applied, Mind Power can bring about almost magical results. But as this businessman will tell you, it's not magic; rather, it's application and technique.

You can experience results of equal significance. Think of your negative programming cycle. Work through an example where your negative thoughts interfered with your desired outcome. Perhaps you choked up on a test, or on the basketball court, or reading a report in front of the class. It doesn't matter what the event was; it happens to everyone. The secret is in being able to recognize the negative programming cycle—those actual negative thoughts that forced you to worry and sabotaged your result.

THE ORIGINS OF NEGATIVE PROGRAMMING

It's interesting how early your tapes can become negatively programmed. The businessman I just referred to could vividly recall being humiliated by his seventh-grade teacher for giggling nervously while attempting to recite a poem in front of the class. That scene controlled his behavior for 27 years! It was classic negative programming that went unattended.

What programming is holding you back? Have you been told you won't amount to anything? Are you telling yourself such garbage? Most people who go through their lives underachieving are burdened with this bad habit— the negative programming cycle, Bad Habit Number 1.

THE NEGATIVE PROGRAMMING CYCLE

Too Much Thinking

|

Negative Thinking

|

Worry

|

Self-limiting Behavior

Your programming cycle is a product of every aspect of your life up to this point. It's learned behavior, a habit that you probably have been unaware of most of the time. Before you panic about your programming cycle, I've got some good news for you. All habits can be changed in only 21 days. You can change a lifetime programming habit within 21 days, if you are aggressively committed to changing. This is where, as a student, you have a significant advantage—you are exposed to learning every day in school. You are about to learn how to make a habit of controlling your internal programming cycle. Let there be no doubt about it—this is STRONG stuff!

From this moment on, realize that your future, your success in the classroom, on the athletic field, socially, with your family and ultimately in your chosen career, will be influenced directly by the decision to control your programming cycle. I will teach you, coach you, show you the way, but you have to make the decision. "I am in control of my future!" needs to be the theme, not "Let me give this a shot and I'll see what happens." Think about your current pattern of thoughts, your present attitude as I outline Success Habit Number 1—the positive programming cycle.

THE POSITIVE PROGRAMMING CYCLE

Goal Thought
|
Repeated
|
Visualized
|
Goal-Compulsive Activities
|
Goal Achievement

Let me repeat: You can't control the thoughts that enter your mind. But your success depends on your ability to control the thoughts you dwell on. These repeated thoughts determine whether you function in a positive or negative programming cycle. It's that simple. Simple, yes. Easy? No change is easy.

The results of the programming cycle you choose can be spectacular! Jeff's story is a perfect example of the power created from this process. A junior in high school, Jeff was brought to me by his mother. She had made the appointment because Jeff was having trouble with his grades. He was on track to fail one course, and possibly another. In talking with Jeff, it became obvious that he was immersed in the negative programming cycle. In one course, he didn't like the teacher, and in the other course he simply hated the subject. Compounding all of this was his mother. Her concern was now being interpreted as negative pressure. She was getting on Jeff's nerves because she was asking questions, as she should, about a very touchy subject. Suddenly, almost out of nowhere, Jeff found himself trapped in a negative programming cycle that was not of his choice.

Has this ever happened to you?

Fortunately, Jeff was fascinated with the idea of mastering Mind Power; thus he was able to immediately recognize the power of this programming process. As he recounted his thoughts about the teacher he disliked, he was able to realize that not only was this having a negative impact on his grade (he was flunking), but it was carrying over to the subject he didn't like and to his relationship with his mother. Jeff realized that this negative programming cycle was spreading like a cancer. What a revelation!

Through this revelation, this personal understanding, Jeff was able to change. Here is a sample of the difference between his negative cycle and the positive cycle he developed into a habit.

Jeff's negative cycle:	"Mr. Jackson's a fool! Nobody will ever learn anything about biology from him."
Jeff's new positive cycle:	"I enjoy the challenge of learning biology and maintaining a B average."

The fact that his grades went up wasn't lost on Jeff, but what impressed him most was his ability to strengthen the strained relationship he had created with his mother. "It's amazing," he told me, "that I have such control over how I get along with my mother. It used to be bad, but now we get along great. I honestly feel responsible for the change."

Well, yes and no. Jeff did change his programming cycle, but his mother was the person who first brought him to my office. They both deserve credit. By focusing on his goal thoughts, Jeff could handle all the little negatives that were associated with his biology teacher without getting off-track. His goals, which involved his grades and his relationship with his mother, were much stronger than the irritations that used to propel him into that negative cycle. He was able to act accordingly.

The rewards of the positive programming cycle are ever-present. Jeff is back on track in school, feeling better about himself, and has established a pattern that will give him an advantage throughout his life—by controlling his programming cycle, he controls his destiny. You can do this too!

DEVELOPING YOUR POSITIVE PROGRAMMING CYCLE

The first step in the process is to reflect on your life and determine what changes would make you more productive. What changes would help you become more successful in school, a stronger person, develop better relationships, or unlock your true athletic potential? Once these changes have been identified, you then write matching self-affirmation statements. For example, if you wanted to improve your ability to recall what you studied during a test, your matching affirmation to assist this change might be, "I have total memory recall." An affirmation statement is simply a self-talk statement worded in such a manner that it is affirming the ideal as if it were reality now. It is the ultimate lie to your subconscious mind—the ultimate good lie! The precise wording is critical because it will determine what you program into your subconscious. Your subconscious is extremely literal—it takes every message at face value. If you tell yourself, "I am no longer self-conscious," your subconscious interprets it as though you are self-conscious. You need to talk to yourself about what you want, as if it were real now. So you say instead, "I am full of confidence."

Properly worded affirmations will enable you to lie to yourself and enjoy the benefits. The most immediate benefit is the boost in self-esteem. The following is a guide to ensuring that your affirmations have maximum impact.

1. **Personal**. Begin each statement with "I am," "I have," "It's easy for me." This will direct your statements internally, as you can affirm change in yourself, but you cannot affirm change in another person.

   Example: Wrong—"My teacher will praise me on my homework assignment."
   Right—"I love doing my homework!"

2. **Positive**. Leave your problems behind! Always word your affirmations by emphasizing what you desire.

Example: Wrong—"I no longer worry about tests."
Right—"I am relaxed, confident, and enjoy the challenge of tests."

3. **Present Tense**. All affirmations must be worded as if they are true now, even though you have yet to accomplish them.

Example: Wrong—"I will become a good student."
Right—"I am a great student!"

4. **Comparison-Free**. You must "tend thy own garden," as Voltaire told us in his masterpiece *Candide*. You can develop a false sense of reality by evaluating yourself in relation to others. Do not compare!

Example: Wrong—"I'm going to get better grades than Mary."
Right—"I am a top honor roll student."

Another good rule to keep in mind when you write your affirmations is to use words of action and emotion whenever appropriate. This will help accelerate the changes. Use words like quick, powerful, terrific, enjoy, love, strong, etc., when writing your own self-affirmations.

Before you begin writing your affirmation statements, it's always a good idea to become aware of your natural pattern of thoughts. We all have negative thoughts, but what's important is to be able to recognize the negative thoughts you dwell on. You need to know your basic thought patterns. If you are unsure, keep a log of every negative thought for a couple of days. I have found that this is usually long enough to expose any patterns and get you started with the appropriate affirmations. Use your

Mind Power Notebook, date a blank a page and title it "Negative Thought Log."

Once you have an idea of your natural thought patterns, I want you to think of seven specific change areas. Why seven? It's the most memorable and powerful number. So why not? You are going to use seven statements to develop your positive programming cycle. This is a very powerful exercise, and I must again emphasize balance in your goals. You need to include statements about your personal life, family, and possible athletic areas, as well as your student affirmations. If you're going to control your programming, you might as well be a well-rounded individual. It's all within your control.

If you don't balance your statements, you can easily focus entirely on being great in one area at the expense of all others. The tragic case of a young gymnast named Christy Henrich (who I will discuss in detail in the next chapter), and her deadly battle with weight is a perfect example. You must grow as a whole person.

So, think of an area of change, and imagine yourself enjoying the change as if it has already occurred. Then write out what you imagined, in your own words, and you have your own personalized affirmation.

EXAMPLES

Change Area: I want to concentrate better when I study.

Image: See yourself studying with total concentration and absorbing knowledge.

Affirmation: I have total concentration and absorb knowledge when studying.

Change Area: I want more confidence.

Image:	See yourself full of confidence in-
	teracting with friends.
Affirmation:	I am full of confidence!

Use this format in your Mind Power Notebook to write your own. Label your pages "Seven Change Area Affirmations." Create seven of these, your own version, fill in the blank Change Area—Image—Affirmation. This will ensure affirmations that match your desired change.

Change Area: _____

_____

Image: _____

Affirmation: _____

_____

_____

The following are sample affirmations that might help get you started. Let me clarify one point about balance and change. One of my affirmations is: "I am a loving, caring husband and father." This does not mean that I'm currently a lousy father; I'm a good father. This affirmation serves as a balance to other more career-focused statements that could possibly move family lower on my subconscious priority list. Because of the power of affirmations, family, spirituality, and health should always be mentioned.

SAMPLE AFFIRMATIONS

School Success:

- I love school!
- I have total concentration and absorb knowledge when studying.

- I have total memory recall when testing.
- I love the challenge of learning and growing!
- I am goal-focused and always working towards my goals.
- I am highly intelligent and fully capable of learning anything.

Family:

- I am loving and caring to all of my family.
- I always make time for my family!
- I have an excellent relationship with my mother and father.
- I always take time to listen to my parents.
- I enjoy helping my parents around the house.
- I enjoy talking with my parents.

Health:

- I am healthy and fit mentally, physically, and spiritually.
- I exercise every day.
- I am in total control of food and drink.
- I sleep soundly every night and wake rested and refreshed.
- I treat my body as if it were my temple.
- I am relaxed, confident, and full of positive energy.

Personal:

- I like myself!
- I live by the golden rule and treat others as I want to be treated.
- I always work to help others feel better about themselves.

- I am full of confidence and always do what is right. ʌ
- I associate only with positive people.
- I am committed to being the best person I can be!

Please understand that the above affirmations are only samples. My intention is to stimulate your thoughts while demonstrating proper wording and structure. In no way are these samples meant to assume any particular lifestyle or family structure. You provide your own personally customized affirmations.

You are now ready to use your personal affirmations to make a self-programming cassette tape. This will become one of your most powerful self-help tools, accelerating the creation of the most important success habit known to mankind: The Positive Programming Cycle!

Keep reading, you're on a roll.

WRAP-UP

- Most people are victims of the negative programming cycle.
- Everybody has negative thoughts but not everybody is in the negative programming cycle.
- The negative programming cycle is Bad Habit Number 1. It holds more people back than all others combined!
- Too much thinking, negative thinking, and worry lead to self-limiting behavior.
- Your most powerful success habit is the Positive Programming Cycle!
- As a student, you are in one the most programmable stages of life.
- Determine the changes you need to become a better student and the person you want to be.

- Design affirmation statements to match and assist the programming of this change into your subconscious.
- Specific wording of your affirmations is critical: personal, present tense, positive and comparison-free.

Chapter 3

Making Your Most Powerful Self-Help Tape

"You cannot always control circumstances. But you can control your own thoughts."
—Charles E. Popplestone

You are now ready to control your internal tapes. The recordings currently playing in your head are playing with such frequency they are close to becoming your permanent internal program. Ugh! This can be very dangerous to your future. Ah-ah, but now you are going to control the programming, and in effect, rerecord any of those negative tapes. This can get exciting—I get fired up just writing about it! Soon you will have the power to change and control your life. This is the ultimate in power!

But simply reading through these exercises, intellectually understanding them, and discussing them with your friends is not enough. If that was the extent of your involvement, you would soon be drawn back by force of habit to your old tapes, thus forfeiting control over your destiny. Not a good choice. I've seen the best intentions go down the drain because of a failure to act on what I'm about to share with you. So, please, put 30 minutes aside and make your tape. Adults will generally need an hour—they're not as technically competent. Ha!

I've been referring to the programming in your subconscious as internal tapes continually playing that determine your behavior. As you have learned in the previous chapter, most people are held back because of one major bad habit—the negative programming cycle. And, typically, this destructive cycle is in its most formative stage during your student years.

As you have just worked through the change area/affirmation exercises, I am certain you were able to understand how the wording of your self-talk impacts your subconscious programming. This is actually all that is necessary to be able to identify your own natural thought pattern and the appropriate change areas. I assume that you have strategically worded matching affirmation statements to maximize the impact on your internal reprogramming. Am I right? I hope so.

You are now sufficiently prepared to change your internal tapes, your programming cycle. How's that for speed learning? Is this change possible? Of course it is. But it is not easy. Very few adults master their internal tapes because of the deadly combination of outside negative forces and the strength of preexisting bad habits. They get easily distracted and give up, usually at the exact point where they need to press on.

Changing the tapes in your mind requires systematic, aggressive action on an emotional level. This is why it is so important to make your own self-programming cassette.

YOUR PERSONAL PROGRAMMING TAPE

Your affirmations, your voice, your mind, your success! Nothing is more powerful than listening to yourself recite strategically spaced and repeated personal statements, statements concerning exactly what you want out of life.

When most people listen to their voice on a recording for the first time, whether it's leaving a message on an answering machine, dictating a letter, or whatever, they immediately dislike how it sounds. This has always amused me because the most powerful medium to our subconscious minds is our own voice.

Think back to the last time you got excited about a certain class. You couldn't really verbalize your feelings out loud because you didn't want to be teased. Yet you were anxious to get to class and learn and maybe even socialize. Can you relate to this scenario? If you can, I'll bet you can hear exactly what you were thinking at the time. You probably didn't give it any thought, but your subconscious mind heard your thoughts as clearly as if you had spoken them out loud. And you probably did well in that class.

Whether it's cursing under your breath, reflectively thinking to yourself, or silent prayer, your subconscious hears your tone of voice, inflection, mood, and sincerity. I am going to give you two statements of opposite emotion. Say them to yourself as if you were thinking of them naturally.

1. "What a beautiful day!"
2. "I wish that creep would stop bothering me!"

What did your mind do? Not only did you hear yourself as if you had said those statements out loud, it was as if you were really stepping outside to a wonderful day, or actually listening to some jerk continue to bore you to death. Right?

Now repeat those same statements, with the same conviction, out loud. Did you feel more powerful in your conviction when you spoke out loud? Could you feel closer to really being there? You can—as can most—because of the addition of the auditory element from self-talk. Your own voice has personal power.

YOUR VOICE IS YOUR MOST POWERFUL MEDIUM

Nothing has more impact on your behavior than you. This is why the best teachers and coaches are able to keep your attention. Their words are able to influence the way you talk to yourself, at least temporarily. For a real experience, spend a few minutes watching one of those television evangelists preaching. Words, used properly, are the fuel to behavior. Yet most often they take the form of an external fuel trying to get you to act for them, not you. You might act on their influence on occasion, but ultimately you will behave in direct accordance to your internal tapes—your programming.

Since your voice has the most impact on you, let's record it on a cassette tape. Yes, a common tape recorder can replace all the external influences I have mentioned. By recording your personalized affirmation statements, with your enthusiasm and emotion, you will be reprogramming while simply walking, jogging, or driving down the highway of life and listening. Your voice, your message, your mind, your future . . . your success journey!

LET'S MAKE A TAPE

You can use the affirmation statements you developed in the previous chapter or you can create new ones, but you will need seven self-affirmation statements. Because you are reading this book to assist you in gaining lifetime control of your most powerful tool—your mind, which impacts every area of your life—it is important to view your affirmation tape as a tool for personal growth, a tool that can provide you with the ultimate in power. It is your call to choose how you want to target this power. But use your common sense: If improving your grades is your number 1 concern, make four of your seven statements pertain to your schoolwork; if it's sports, weight your affirmations accordingly. Regardless of how you are targeting your ultimate power, and because this is power, make sure to save enough affirmations to ensure balance in your life: personal, family, athletic, spiritual, etc. A good rule of thumb is to always save three affirmations to balance this power.

I am repeating myself because of the power involved with the tool you are about to create. I know it's hard to imagine anything that powerful, but this tool is that powerful! It would be unethical for me to share this exercise with you without insisting upon balance. You're about to get involved with a tool that must be used properly; it's very important to have both balance and control in your life.

This tape will have such an impact that if you fail to incorporate balance into the recording you run the risk of ruining your life. Nothing illustrates this better than the tragic death of world-class gymnast Christy Henrich, whom I mentioned in the previous chapter. Tragic Christy died at age 22 from a complete breakdown of her body's organ system. Her eating habits changed as the result of words she overheard, external forces. A judge suggested that she was too fat to make the Olympic team. The impact on her self-talk and subsequent behavior change transformed her reality from the healthy world of gymnastics into the deathtrap of anorexia nervosa and bulimia. In counseling work, I never allow anyone to make this important tape without including balance.

I call this self-programming cassette your 7-7-7 Tape. How's that for exploiting the magic of the number seven? Essentially, it is seven affirmation statements repeated seven times, with each repetition spaced seven seconds apart. Your entire tape will consist of 49 statements— seven different statements repeated seven times each.

Now what is the purpose of this spaced repetition? Why seven statements? Why seven seconds apart? Since your mind thinks in images and you converse in words, the seven-second pause between repetitions allows your mind to naturally create the images of the affirmation you've just recited. Then by repeating that same affirmation seven seconds later with another seven-second pause, your corresponding images not only become much stronger, they begin to have a reprogramming effect on your subconscious.

Repetition has often been said to be the mother of learning. With that in mind, consider spaced repetition as the father of rescripting the tapes in your mind. If you start repeating more than seven statements, there is a chance you will be confusing yourself and losing the emotional impact of this powerful exercise.

Once, during a series of workshops I was conducting for a sales organization, one of the participants returned to a follow-up workshop with 18 affirmation statements. The other salespeople had developed the seven statements they were going to record during the workshop, as they were making their 7-7-7 Tapes during this particular session. But this individual claimed he needed so much reprogramming that it would be impossible for him to work with any less than 18. So I asked him to share with the group, from memory, his 18 statements. He could only remember seven. My point was made and these seven became the affirmations on his 7-7-7 Tape.

There is magic in the number seven, but also understand that keeping seven repetitions with seven-second spacing linked to your seven affirmation statements adds an element of simplicity. Quite frankly, it is easier for people to remember. You could repeat each statement nine times and pause for ten seconds between. But seven repetitions and seven-second pauses provide the impact necessary for serious rescripting. This will leave you with, approximately, a 10-to-15-minute recording. If you cut back on the number of repetitions or shorten the pauses, you would lessen the impact on your subconscious mind. Your objective is to maximize the impact! Keep with 7-7-7.

DOES THIS REALLY WORK?

Many people initially categorize this 7-7-7 Tape with the subliminal tapes that are sold today everywhere. This is a big mistake. First of all, the concept behind a subliminal message is that it is not audible on a conscious level, but rather on a preconscious level. Although there is validity to that concept, two concerns immediately surface:

1. The validity of the program you purchase. For those who wish to purchase the subliminal product, I recommend Denis Waitley's *The Subliminal Winner*, produced by Nightingale Conant, or Dr. Maxwell Maltz's *Pyscho-Cybernetics*. Both are credible.
2. The most powerful programming tool for your mind is your message, your self-talk, and your voice. I've met thousands of people who wasted money on subliminal products because they expected the tapes to automatically make a change in their lives. This never happens!

What about sleep learning? Let me share with you an overview of a sleep-learning experiment conducted in Bulgaria in the late '60s that was reported by Sheila Ostrander and Lynn Schroeder in their book *Superlearning*. Dr. Georgi Lazanov, a Bulgarian doctor and psychiatrist, became fascinated with the concept of learning. He was convinced that human beings were using only a fraction of their mental capacities. His life's journey became a study of the human learning process. While on this journey he was exposed to a technique called sleep learning. Pioneered by the Russians, it was then making headlines in the United States.

He set out to test this learning phenomenon himself. Taking a group of students, Dr. Lazanov carefully explained how their lessons of that particular day were going to be reinforced by special sleep-learning recordings as they slept that evening. And on that evening, as the students slept, Dr. Lazanov divided them into two groups by disconnecting the sleep-learning recordings for half the students, unbeknownst to any of them. They all assumed they were getting their lessons reinforced while they slept.

The following day all the students were tested. Guess what? They all scored higher. There was no difference between the students who listened to the sleep-learning message and those who only thought they did. The conclusion was that merely the suggestion of enhanced learning had impacted both groups to pay more attention during their lessons and have better memory recall the following day.

Learning can be reinforced during sleep, but it is not a panacea. The equipment is cumbersome and difficult to time properly and one never has control of his or her memory recall, and thus it is rarely used.

For Susan, an adult continuing-education student, recording and listening to an affirmation tape saved her from terrible grades. She was suffering from pre-test anxiety. Her mind began functioning in a negative cycle where she saw her entire career going down the tubes because of her inability to take tests. She knew she was capable, but she had been out of the classroom/testing mode for over 20 years and was unsure of her ability to perform.

I was able to get Susan to recognize her role in applying Mind Power to her studies. Frustrated by the lack of results from a sleep-learning tape she purchased through a mail-order ad, her confidence was going down along with her grades. It was only after I explained the realities of sleep learning that I was able to convince her she could reprogram the tapes in her head towards studying and testing. Out of desperation she followed my advice, my studying and testing tactics (which I'll get into later), and she made a self-affirmation tape.

Three days after her first appointment she experienced the power of being directly involved with her mind—she got an "A" on a test. She went on to pass her real estate course, received her license, and now uses another self-affirmation tape to help her sell houses. Let me take you through four simple steps that will enable you to make your self-affirmation tape.

FOUR STEPS—STEP BY STEP

I have listed seven affirmation statements in the format I want you to use when you write yours in your Mind Power Notebook. Title a blank page "7-7-7 Tape" and write the date next to it. Every time you change your tape, list all seven statements and make certain you date the change. This will help keep you organized. Use the following affirmations as examples; if some of the statements reflect your needs, feel free to use them. But please put thought into your statements No two people will have identical Mind Power needs. Your tape should reflect you and your needs. This is what will make it most powerful and effective. Eventually you'll reach Susan's level, where you can make tapes for other areas of your life.

Step 1: Write out seven self-affirmation statements.

1. I enjoy learning!
2. I have total concentration and absorb knowledge when studying!

3. I am alert, attentive, and make a positive contribution in class!
4. I always do my homework every night!
5. I am healthy and fit mentally, physically, and spiritually!
6. I am loving and caring to my family and friends!
7. I am full of confidence and positive energy!

Step 2: **Test your voice for clarity, volume, and cadence. Record your first statement three times, just as if you were making the entire tape:** I enjoy learning! (1-2-3-4-5-6-7) I enjoy learning! (1-2-3-4-5-6-7) I enjoy learning! (1-2-3-4-5-6-7)

Step 3: **Replay your recorded affirmations and make the proper adjustments.**

1. Speak slowly in a clear, audible manner.
2. Speak slightly louder than normal conversational tone.
3. Change your voice inflection to enhance the images created.
4. Use the second hand of a clock, a digital watch, or simply count to seven for timing your pauses.

Step 4: **Record your 7-7-7 Self-Programming Tape.** *Note:* The following example will use the seven affirmation statements above.

1. I enjoy learning! (1-2-3-4-5-6-7) I enjoy learning! (1-2-3-4-5-6-7) I enjoy learning! (1-2-3-4-5-6-7) I enjoy learning! (1-2-3-4-5-6-7) I enjoy learning! (1-2-3-4-5-6-7) I enjoy learning! (1-2-3-4-5-6-7) I enjoy learning! (1-2-3-4-5-6-7)
2. I have total concentration and absorb knowledge when studying! (1-2-3-4-5-6-7) I have total concentration and absorb knowledge when studying!

(1-2-3-4-5-6-7) I have total concentration and absorb knowledge when studying! (1-2-3-4-5-6-7) I have total concentration and absorb knowledge when studying! (1-2-3-4-5-6-7) I have total concentration and absorb knowledge when studying! (1-2-3-4-5-6-7) I have total concentration and absorb knowledge when studying! (1-2-3-4-5-6-7) I have total concentration and absorb knowledge when studying! (1-2-3-4-5-6-7)

3. Continue this process for all seven statements. Let this 7-7-7 Self-Programming Tape serve as a passive tool while you're walking, jogging, or driving or involved in other activities. You don't have to listen to every word. This is the magic of this rescripting tool—your conscious mind can be drifting off to other thoughts as you listen, but your subconscious will always be creating those powerful images.

You never have to force your images. The spacing is designed for the images to occur naturally, and they will. At times, you will find yourself paying closer attention without conscious effort; on other occasions, your mind will wander. Let it, this is only normal. As long as you listen to the tape on a daily basis, you will rescript your mind on an emotional level. You will be taking a major shortcut in changing the tapes that govern your life.

For those who appreciate music and understand the high-tech world of electronics, you may enjoy recording your affirmations over music. Make certain you select a relaxing instrumental, otherwise the music might become a distraction. But with the proper selection of music, you can make magic. The most powerful 7-7-7 Tapes I've had the pleasure of listening to have all used relaxing music. If you can forget about stereophonic sound and keep focused only on reprogramming, all that is necessary is to play your music on one system, mono, sit by a speaker with the machine you are using to record your affirmations, and do it. You will make a powerful tape!

REPROGRAM EVERY 21 DAYS

Since it takes 21 days of aggressive activity to change a habit, I have found it most effective to change the tape every 21 days. I know, this requires time and energy. But that is exactly what is going to contribute to ultimate success!

I've discovered over the years of working with students in making their personal 7-7-7 Tapes that the initial excitement sometimes turns into boredom. Some people get tired of hearing the same message, especially if they have grown beyond some of their original affirmations.

Certain affirmation statements will probably always remain constant. For example, "I am always learning, growing, and accepting challenges!" and "I live by the golden rule and always do what is right!" could always provide benefit. Two affirmations I always personally keep are: "I am healthy and fit mentally, physically, and spiritually!" and "I am a loving, caring husband and father!" Through this process you will always control your internal tapes, and therefore always continue to challenge yourself. Once you master a change area, it's time to find another change area and record another tape.

THIRD-PERSON PROGRAMMING

For those of you who really enjoy the idea of being at the controls of your own programming, third-person affirmation statements are a tremendous boost. After you finish recording your forty-ninth statement, you can fill the remainder of the cassette side with compliments about yourself. For example:

> You're the best! (1-2-3-4-5-6-7) You're the best! (1-2-3-4-5-6-7)
> You are an excellent student! etc.
> You always do what is right! etc.

And so on. . . . Each third-person affirmation should be repeated at least twice. Few students receive enough compliments, so why not compliment yourselves? Many students enjoy the third-person affirmation so much that they make an entire tape of third-person compliments.

Remember, the better you feel about yourself the more successful you will be. Proactive people aren't going to wait for their parents, teachers, coaches, neighbors, or friends to make them feel good; they are going to do that themselves—hence the value of third-person affirmations. These are really compliments to yourself that you would love to receive. So go ahead now and receive them!

WRAP-UP

- Nothing is more powerful than the thoughts you repeat in your mind.
- You can reprogram your mind through affirmations.
- Affirmations are basically self-talk in the present tense, in a positive, personal, and comparison-free form.
- Your voice is your most powerful programming medium.
- Seven affirmations are the most effective number to program at one time.

- Follow the Four Steps in recording your 7-7-7 Tape.
- Remake your tape every 21 days.
- Third-person programming is powerful—"You're the best!"

Chapter 4

Role Model Power

"The price of greatness is responsibility."
                    —Winston Churchill

Nike once paid NBA superstar Charles Barkley an outrageous sum to snarl into a television camera, "I'm not a role model. Parents are role models." My response is simple, "Yeah, right!" Sure, parents are the primary role models in life. But the reality is that much of your development will come from modeling attitudes and behaviors of people other than your parents. Which is exactly why Nike and other major companies spend millions of dollars to have athletes like Charles Barkley "pitch" their products.

Role Model Power is awesome. It can lead you down a path of either constructive or destructive Mind Power—without you ever realizing what's happening. I can remember as a senior at the University of Arizona spending every lunch period in the weight room with a buddy. We worked out hard, knew everyone who regularly lifted and their workout routine. During one lunchtime workout something occurred that had an impact on me for the next twenty years.

A new face appeared in the gym. No big deal, except the face belonged to one of the university's professors. I had never seen him without a shirt and tie. He was wearing shorts and a tank top. Guessing his age to be mid-forties, I watched him out of the corner of my eye. He proceeded to lift 150 pounds over his head and knock off two quick sets of triceps curls—that's an exercise where you hold your hands close together in the middle of the bar with the weight over your head and slowly lower the weight behind your head and then push it back up. If I've lost you on this, take my word for it—it's hard to do this exercise with a lot less than 150 pounds.

Instantly I decided to be in the same shape when I was forty. I never saw this professor in the weight room again, as he must have had a different exercise schedule, but the image of a suit-and-tie professional being in such good shape stayed with me. I compared him to other people who I figured to be in their forties. There was no comparison, not even with the athletic coaches. From then on, almost without realizing it, I used my mind even more constructively regarding my own strength and fitness. I was beginning with the end in mind. Not that forty is the end, but for a twenty-year-old it was pretty far off into the future.

A few years ago I reached this date with destiny; I turned forty. About six months before the big day, with my fitness role model locked in my mind, I set two goals to be accomplished on my fortieth birthday. Determined to put an end to all the "You're over the hill" teasing and model my hero, I intended to bench-press 225 pounds for ten repetitions and do 40 pull-ups (35 was the most I'd ever done). You may be bored listening to my training, which included self-affirmations on my tape and a shoulder injury from lifting without the proper warm-up. But on my fortieth birthday I did it. I accomplished my goal and now I see myself as a role model similar to the professor who made such an impression on me.

Whether you realize it or not, Role Model Power has a constant impact on everyone. One of the more effective ways to gain an understanding of the awesome power of role models is to study the uninhibited phase of human learning and growth—the infant. A life of pure energy, a tiny baby is like a fresh sponge, absorbing all the stimuli of his or her little world. Naturally gathering and storing information through sight, touch, sound, movement, and energy, an infant is free from the encumbrance of opinions, attitudes, and self-limiting beliefs. There are no internal tapes inside this little creature.

Often without any awareness, parents immediately take on nature's designation as role models for their children. Only you can decide whether your parents have understood this responsibility. You might not believe this, but you probably already share many mannerisms and habits of your parents. A radio interview I once did in Los Angeles illustrates this all too clearly.

YOUR PARENTS' ROLE

The topic of this radio interview was a book I'd written, *The Autohypnosis Diet*. Essentially Mind Power was the topic and I had a good dialogue going with an informed host of a popular call-in talk show. One of the call-ins came from four young teenage girls who claimed to be overweight. They wanted a few tips on mental training to lose weight. It just so happened the radio station was in a shopping mall and they were calling from a phone booth in the same mall. The talk show host invited them to visit us in the studio. A few minutes later four attractive young teenagers walked into the room. We looked at each other as if this was some sort of a practical joke—four teenage girls putting one over on us. But they were deadly serious! It was strange talking with four thin teenagers about their weight. Not one was close to being overweight. When I steered the conversation towards their parents, all had at least one parent obsessed with weight.

Role Model Power was at work as these parents unwittingly passed this destructive mind-set on to their daughters. What is really scary is that these girls were on the road to creating similar eating disorders to the one that killed Christy Henrich. You might know someone who suffers from anorexia or bulimia. The power of role models is awesome, both constructively and destructively.

Have you ever given much thought to the habits, attitudes, and behaviors that you have acquired from your parents? Think of some your parents' attitudes and behaviors that drive you crazy. Are they always late? Maybe they don't listen to what you're really saying. Maybe they are overly critical. Whatever they are, if you're really honest with yourself there is a good chance you'll notice similar tendencies developing in yourself. Similarly, think of some of the good habits your parents possess. Good manners, good eating and exercise habits . . . you are likely to follow this model that is being established before you.

All of us have picked up habits, good and bad, from our parents. In the past you might have been blind to this. Most students are, especially when it comes to those destructive tendencies. But this is merely a defense mechanism. It's not pleasant to think about negative attitudes and behaviors that mirror those of your parents. It becomes easier to be more objective when you observe a brother or sister. But please realize that you are no different. We are all creatures of habit and all habits are learned.

Extensive research by family therapists indicates conclusively that negative behavior is learned and passed on from generation to generation. Dr. Susan Forward in her book *Toxic Parents* cites numerous cases where a parent who was verbally abused as a child verbally abuses her own children. Dr. Forward writes of adults beaten by a parent as a child beating their own children.

I sincerely hope this is not your case. But I have worked with numerous individuals suffering from low self-esteem and poor self-image because of poor attitudes and habits learned from parents. In each instance, these sufferers could list their parents' character flaws and vowed never to acquire those destructive traits. Alas, they did not un-derstand how to use Mind Power or Role Model Power and they acquired exactly what they vowed to avoid.

CREATING YOUR POSITIVE ROLE MODEL

You must begin with the end in mind. Think of your crystal ball exercise. As you visualize these achievements, think of someone who already embodies what you are about to achieve—much as I did with that professor who lifted weights at the University of Arizona. I never knew the man but was thoroughly impressed with his image, so I created a model in my mind of what I thought he was like; a man who made a living with his brain but who also kept his body in top shape. This was the end I had in mind. You can do the same.

Whenever you begin with the end in mind you elimi-nate confusion. There is always that pressure to hang out and play games—some students even drop out. But when you start with the end in mind and fast-forward these peo-ple to the age of forty, the picture gets quite ugly and it's hard to think of these people as being very cool. Stupid maybe. This little exercise in forward thinking can pro-vide clarity to your vision.

I grew up in White Plains, New York, which is a north-ern suburb of New York City. Although it wasn't the Big Apple, we had direct access to the city and used it regu-larly. Two incidents come to mind and both occurred dur-ing summer jobs. The first involved a tough older kid who was working on the loading docks where I got my first summer job. It was with a moving company. This older kid—he was all of seventeen—took a liking to me and tried to talk me into getting a tattoo, just like his. Some-how my father got wind of this and simply asked me to look at someone who was forty and had a tattoo. That's all I needed.

A few summers later, as I worked my way up the ladder and began driving these moving vans, the owner tried to talk me into quitting college and driving full-time. I was making a lot of money on a part-time basis and knew two students who had taken a similar offer the previous year. They were now full-time moving van drivers, making good money—both had recently purchased new Corvettes.

Once again, my father, one of my strongest role models, entered the picture. Planting seeds, beginning with the end in mind, he simply asked me to examine the educational levels of adults who I knew personally and admired. The deck was stacked; he knew full well how much I admired our extended family, many of whom just happened to be successful lawyers. There is nothing wrong with being a professional truck driver—and I never did become an attorney—but with that simple directive, my father forced me to simultaneously use role models and think with the end in mind. I quickly realized that continuing my education was going to help me get more of what I wanted out of life.

Behind every high achiever is usually a positive role model. You can refer to this person as a mentor, hero, teacher, coach, mother, father . . . the label is not important. What is important is realizing that you can accelerate your positive growth by identifying with such a role model.

Do you have a positive hero? Do you have a constructive role model? The following is an exercise that can help get you started. I want you to determine all of the constructive and destructive habits you have acquired from your parents. The following is an example:

Constructive Acquired Habits

- Personal hygiene
- Strong discipline

- Good manners
- Honesty
- Thirst for learning
- Reading
- Sense of humor
- Self-confidence

Destructive Acquired Habits

- Worry
- Low self-esteem
- Bad eating habits
- Too much television
- Bad temper
- Negative attitude
- Laziness
- Poor manners

The above is just a sampling to give you an idea of what I want you to look for. The objective of this exercise is twofold. You will more fully understand the power of role models and you'll begin to break away from habits that might be holding you back.

Get out your Mind Power Notebook, turn to a blank page, and write "Constructive Acquired Habits" at the top. Then spend between fifteen and thirty minutes listing all of your good habits. Whether they're table manners, study habits, hygiene . . . relax and spend some time listing your good habits.

Next, go to another blank page and write "Destructive Acquired Habits" at the top. Hopefully, this will be a much more difficult exercise, as your list won't be nearly as long. Nevertheless, you have acquired some bad habits. 'Fess up, put them on paper, as you're getting ready to free yourself of these destructive habits.

What's sad is that most people go through life without

a positive hero. And too many kids model destructive forces simply because they do not start with the end in mind. Ask your parents about their role models, but don't be surprised if you get a blank stare. Most adults don't have a positive role model. Yet many high achievers do. . . .

Michael Jordan patterned his basketball game after two local stars, David Thompson and Walter Davis. They were his inspiration to excel, to dunk, and to make it to the NBA after getting cut from his high school team. One of the great American leaders during World War II, General George Patton, idolized Alexander the Great. As a youth, George Patton studied everything ever written about his hero. When he was a cadet at West Point he patterned his military career after Alexander. When General Patton was in the heat of battle against the Nazis in Europe, all his decisions were made with the consideration of how his role model Alexander the Great would have acted under similar circumstances. A cynic might say it's a coincidence that neither general lost a battle. I would have to disagree.

Your constructive role model can come from anywhere. You can use history, like General Patton, contemporaries as did Michael Jordan, or both. There can never be a shortage of positive role models. I consider myself extremely fortunate to count both my mother and father as role models. Yet, being a lover of history, I've gotten many role models from history books as well. Take Abraham Lincoln as just one example. His leadership during our country's most bitter conflict is common knowledge. Because of this he is one of my role models and is worthy of in-depth study. Let me share with you the role model exercise, using Lincoln, as I want you to complete with one of your positive role models.

ROLE MODEL: Abraham Lincoln

Qualities and Characteristics

- Honest
- Disciplined
- Self-taught
- Hard-working
- Considerate
- Overcame adversity
- Outstanding public speaker
- Goal-focused visionary
- Practical/common sense
- Loyal
- Student of history

I could go on, but hopefully you get the idea. Listing the qualities and characteristics of someone you truly admire, beginning with the end in mind, will provide a powerful roadmap for your personal development. You will never become your role models, but you might even surpass their accomplishments.

YOUR POSITIVE ROLE MODEL

Once again, turn to another blank page in your trusted Mind Power Notebook and write ''Positive Role Model'' at the top. Under this label, using one individual at a time, write the name of this particular role model and the corresponding qualities and characteristics that make your hero special. As you follow this format with each role model, something interesting should occur. Many of the qualities and characteristics will be the same. You will have discovered what most people never fully recognize: the common denominator of high achievers.

From this exercise you can create specific affirmations using some of the qualities you have highlighted in your role models. Have fun with this. If you dare, you might consider sharing this exercise with your parents and teachers. Ask about their role models. Don't be surprised if the answer takes the form of a blank stare.

Many studies of high achievers have been conducted, but few have defined high achievement. For the purposes of mastering Mind Power, it's important to narrow the field and create a specific template with which to model. The definition I have selected is a modified version created at Harvard, Stanford, Yale, and the University of Massachusetts as the result of a research project on high achievers in which these institutions collaborated. First, it is important to understand the definition that was applied to "high achiever." The following is my wording of the definition.

> HIGH ACHIEVER: "An individual who has incorporated balance in his or her life; continuing to grow, set and achieve goals, live by the golden rule, and add value to work, family, and community."

This sets a lofty standard, I know, but the objective is not simply to make a lot of money or be a professional athlete. No! The objective is to be a good person who goes through life's journey committed to growth and giving— to create a life.

As you read through these qualities, the idea is to conduct an informal comparative analysis with one of your role models. Think of how your role model would respond to each quality, and then ask yourself, "How do I rate?" Write the name of your role model in the space above this exercise and then select the number most applicable for both you and your role model for all 15 qualities, with 1 being a quality least like you and 10 being most like you. Although you will be only speculating with your role model's scoring, it is important to be honest with yourself during this exercise.

Role Model _____

1. **Balanced Lifestyle:** Our high achievers have
   full lives, paying attention to personal, professional, and spiritual development; family, career, and religion.

   > 1 2 3 4 5 6 7 8 9 10

   Role Model:
   You:

2. **Goal-focused:** High achievers have a strong
   sense of purpose and work their life from a specific plan. They control as much as they can.

   > 1 2 3 4 5 6 7 8 9 10

   Role Model:
   You:

3. **Delay Gratification:** High achievers fully understand the law of the harvest: seeds planted
   today must be carefully tended to bear fruit tomorrow. They are able to work hard for a goal
   that will provide rewards far off in the future
   rather than living in the world of immediate
   gratification.

   > 1 2 3 4 5 6 7 8 9 10

   Role Model:
   You:

4. **Optimistic:** Positive thinking is a common denominator in high achievers. Because of their
   goal focus they can not afford to be negative or
   burdened with excessive worry, but at the same
   time they are realistic.

   > 1 2 3 4 5 6 7 8 9 10

   Role Model:
   You:

5. **Confident:** High achievers have the confidence to forge ahead without needing the approval of their peers, which is essential since most of their peers are probably not high achievers. High achievers have complete belief in their ability, often without any proof, to achieve their goals.

    1 2 3 4 5 6 7 8 9 10

    Role Model:
    You:

6. **High Self-esteem:** Self-esteem continues to grow as you grow and achieve. It is no coincidence that high achievers have high self-esteem—they earned it. So will you.

    1 2 3 4 5 6 7 8 9 10

    Role Model:
    You:

7. **Positive Self-image:** These people have the ability to see themselves as successful well in advance of their actual achievements. Their positive self-image is in harmony with their goals.

    1 2 3 4 5 6 7 8 9 10

    Role Model:
    You:

8. **Self-discipline:** All high achievers possess the magic of self-motivation; this is discipline. Linked to goals, success naturally follows. Good study habits, good work habits, exercise habits, etc., are all elements of self-discipline.

    1 2 3 4 5 6 7 8 9 10

    Role Model:
    You:

9. **Role Models' Role:** High achievers actively model themselves after people they admire, successful people, and eventually become role models for others.

   1 2 3 4 5 6 7 8 9 10

   Role Model:
   You:

10. **Empowerment:** These individuals traditionally bring out the best in the people around them by helping them believe in themselves. They are active sources of encouragement.

    1 2 3 4 5 6 7 8 9 10

    Role Model:
    You:

11. **Avoid Negative Influences:** Misery loves company, but high achievers have learned to avoid such company at all costs. Achievers associate with achievers. They avoid negative people like the plague.

    1 2 3 4 5 6 7 8 9 10

    Role Model:
    You:

12. **Courage:** Nothing ventured, nothing gained is the motto for high achievers. They take risks and are willing to fail in order to succeed. Winston Churchill said it best: "Courage is the first of human qualities because it is the quality which guarantees all the others."

    1 2 3 4 5 6 7 8 9 10

    Role Model:
    You:

13. **Health and Fitness:** People who get the most out of life need high levels of energy. Thus they

have developed the proper eating, sleeping, and exercise habits. They rarely get sick and can not afford needless fatigue.

1 2 3 4 5 6 7 8 9 10

Role Model:
You:

14. **Persistent:** Ben Franklin termed it resolution. High achievers finish what they start and work diligently, sometimes against great odds, day after day. They do not make excuses.

1 2 3 4 5 6 7 8 9 10

Role Model:
You:

15. **Golden Rule:** Our high achievers treated people the way they would like to be treated. Their success was not at the expense of other people.

1 2 3 4 5 6 7 8 9 10

Role Model:
You:

There are other qualities that you might have included, such as kindness, spiritual life, family orientation, to name a few, but this list is actually more complete than it might appear to be at first glance. Keep in mind that the intention is to highlight the human qualities which represent the person you want to become. The next chapter will continue the process of beginning with the end in mind as you will be creating your own Master Dream List. Hey, if you are going to control your life and master Mind Power, you might as well be going after real dreams.

WRAP-UP

- Role models are either positive or negative.
- Your most accelerated growth comes from following role models.
- Parents are your initial role models.
- You have already acquired many habits from your parents.
- Select a positive role model.
- Identify your negative acquired habits that you need to correct.
- What positive acquired habits are you going to further enhance?

Chapter 5

Life Mapping: Your Master Dream List

"The future belongs to those who believe in the beauty of their dreams."

—Eleanor Roosevelt

Many years ago a teenage boy stumbled onto an exercise that should be required of every human being, as it would force people to get more out of life. It was a rainy Sunday morning back in 1940, when a bookish, imaginative fifteen-year-old John Goddard decided to list all the things he wanted to do during his life. He pondered for some time, then carefully wrote 127 goals on a pad of yellow paper under the title "John Goddard's Master Dream List." The following partial list will give you an idea of the magnitude of Goddard's imagination.

Rivers to Navigate:

1. Nile River
2. Amazon River
3. Congo River
4. Colorado River
5. Yangtze River
6. Niger River
7. Orinoco River, Venezuela
8. Rio Coco, Nicaragua

Study Primitive Cultures in:

9. The Congo
10. New Guinea
11. Brazil
12. Borneo
13. The Sudan
14. Australia
15. Kenya
16. The Philippines
17. Tanganyika
18. Ethiopia
19. Nigeria
20. Alaska

Mountains to Climb:

21. Mt. Everest
22. Mt. Aconcagua, Argentina
23. Mt. McKinley
24. Mt. Huascarán, Peru
25. Mt. Kilimanjaro
26. Mt. Ararat, Turkey
27. Mt. Kenya

John's list was adventuresome, to say the least, but he had created a master plan for his life. What was unique about Goddard's plan was that it became a blueprint for an incredible life journey.

"When I was 15," he told *Life* magazine's Richard Woodbury, "all the adults I knew seemed to complain, 'Oh, if only I'd done this or that when I was younger.' They had let life slip by them. I was sure that if I planned for it, I could have a life of excitement and fun and knowledge." (Richard Woodbury, "One Man's Life of No Regrets," *Life*, March 24, 1972)

The earlier accomplishments were the easier ones: learning how to type, becoming an Eagle Scout (number

73), but after college (he studied premed and eventually treated illnesses among primitive tribes—number 37) and a hitch in the air force (numbers 40 and 75), he began pursuing goals in earnest. In the early 1950s, he became the first man to explore the entire length of the Nile by kayak (number 1); that celebrated expedition established him as an adventurer-lecturer.

Healthy and fit even after reaching middle age (number 102), Goddard continued his quests of climbing, studying, visiting, and exploring. He was nearly buried alive in a Sudanese sandstorm (number 13). He was chased by a warthog while photographing Victoria Falls (number 43). He saw the Pope at the Vatican (number 59). He was bitten by a diamondback rattlesnake during a photo session while milking the reptile (number 117). He traveled around the globe four times (number 124).

John Goddard died in Africa during 1971, but not before completing 103 of the 127 dreams from his master list. Many people have followed Goddard's ambitious example. Notre Dame football coach Lou Holtz is noted for carry his dream list with him wherever he goes. How about you?

YOUR MASTER DREAM LIST

Start with the end in mind. First think of how long you would like to live. Interestingly, the older someone gets, the longer they plan on living. I guess people become wiser with age. The truth is that it's wiser to plan on living a long, healthy life at a young age. Once you have determined your longevity, it's time to dream a little. What would you ideally like to accomplish? Remember, Goddard started off with accomplishments such as becoming an Eagle Scout, college, and premed. His more adventurous dreams were accomplished later in life. What is important, he developed the habit of going after his dreams.

As you prepare to do the same, it is helpful to break your dream list into four basic categories of accomplishments; professional, personal, family, and spiritual. Consider your education and career path as part of your professional dream accomplishments. Your health, travel, hobbies, etc., would be more personal. Family could also be considered personal, but it involves other people—just ask your folks. Your spiritual life should be the fabric that connects all your dreams. Ultimately, you are planning more than your temporary visit on this planet we call Earth. Right?

FIRST THINGS FIRST

As you create your master plan, your Master Dream List, serious consideration must be given to immediate upcoming accomplishments. These are the first steps linking you to your plan. Whether it's increasing your grades, getting a specific score on the SATs, graduating from college, getting into graduate school, or going back to school—first things first. You might change various aspects of your master plan, future accomplishments might change in importance, but the immediate future should be rather simple to prioritize.

Recently I purchased a notebook computer which would allow me to bring my work, write this book, wherever I traveled. Because I was completely focused on my goal of finishing this book, putting first things first, I jumped right into my project, writing away using my antiquated word-processing software, without taking the time to learn how to use all the bells and whistles bundled into the new toy, excuse me, tool. When working from a plan, it becomes very natural to remember your immediate priorities—it's your link to your master plan.

Now that you've got a real hero, a high achiever template to model, coupled with the fact that you know how to control the programming powers of your mind, you are prepared to become that person you want to be. This is where it becomes important to begin applying all these positive steps to a Master Dream List. I call this linking.

You don't have to be as ambitious as John Goddard with your Master Dream List. Few people are. But I do recommend thinking of between five to ten accomplishments per category. This is to be a living, breathing document. In other words, you can add or delete from your list at any time. Here is an example of a good initial Master Dream List.

Professional:

1. Get accepted into the University of Arizona
2. Graduate Magna Cum Laude with a BS in archeology
3. Spend one year on an archeological dig in Central America
4. Attend graduate school and get a PhD in archeology
5. Teach archeology at the university level
6. Lead a major archeological dig

Personal:

1. Bench-press 250 pounds and do 25 chin-ups
2. Complete a marathon
3. Make the debate team
4. Broadcast a college baseball game
5. Spend a summer backpacking through Europe
6. Attend a game at every major league baseball stadium
7. Live a healthy and full life beyond age 95

Family:

1. Be happily married by age 30
2. Have three healthy, wonderful children by age 40
3. Have a close relationship with parents, brothers, and sisters
4. Have an annual family reunion
5. Raise children to be healthy, full-functioning, self-sufficient adults
6. Keep the romance in my marriage
7. Live on a 20-acre ranch in Arizona
8. Achieve total financial freedom by age 40

Spiritual:

1. I continue to strengthen my belief
2. I make a pilgrimage to the Holy Land
3. I instill strong spiritual beliefs and values into my children
4. I am always actively involved in whatever church I attend
5. I teach Bible studies
6. I live by the Golden Rule

You get the idea. When thinking first things first, every activity must be linked to an objective, which in turn is linked to a master plan. For example, high school grades and SAT scores are linked to admissions to the college of choice, course selection and grades in college are linked to career choice/graduate school, career choice/graduate school is linked to a future lifestyle for a lifetime, and so on. Every serious decision should be linked to this master plan—your Master Dream List. Now don't let this appear overwhelming—it's really only common sense.

YOUR MASTER DREAM LIST

Okay, let's have some fun and dream a little. Your only requirement is to allow me to guide you into adding a bit of structure to the process. Get your trusted Mind Power Notebook, turn to two blank facing pages, and title this section "Master Dream List." Directly under this heading, write today's date, your age and the age you ideally would like to live. So you might be 21 years old today and would love to live to be 101 years old. Keep in mind, the age you select is outside your direct control, but it serves a purpose. It helps you begin with the end in mind as you create your Master Dream List.

Now you want to divide your dream list into the four categories already discussed: professional, personal, family, and spiritual. Allow a half-page for each category. Now start dreaming, beginning with the end in mind. Take your time with this. You can add to this list, delete dreams and modify dreams. The idea is to get you thinking into your future. In the next chapter you will learn how to prioritize your dreams into immediate accomplishments, such as grades, SAT scores, college acceptance, etc., but before you get involved with current goals, it's important to begin the process of establishing a Master Dream List. This will allow you to link your immediate objectives to a master plan.

Most people don't work from such a plan. They never had a dream list. Most of your teachers, parents, aunts, and uncles have simply gone through life as it appeared to them, one isolated decision at the time. Thus many of their major decisions were in conflict with what they really wanted out of life. Dropping out of college, getting messed up with drugs, breaking the law, taking a job with no future but a decent paycheck today, marrying too early, having children without planning for a family, etc.—all are examples of isolated decisions that are not linked to any type of Master Dream List. Your decisions however, will be linked to a plan—your Master Dream List.

Mind Power for students is far more than simply learning how to use your mind more constructively. It is about grabbing the controls of your life at an early age, thus avoiding the mistakes that have derailed so many adults from living their dreams. I believe that one of the reasons so many people fail in using self-help materials is because they never linked their personal development to a master plan. They lack clear-cut goals. My work with students tells me one of the reasons so many struggle with studies in both high school and college is because they have no master plan, no goal; they have not linked all of this hard work to anything.

None of this is new. Once you have created a master plan, in essence you have established a way in which you can mold clear-cut goals. As you begin following your master plan, going after your goals, there is a definition of success in the form of a poem which can serve as your theme. It's a verse entitled "Achievement," which was written many years ago by Robert Louis Stevenson, author of many classics, including the popular volumes *Treasure Island* and *Kidnapped*. Read this passage out loud, allow your imagination to see the pictures Stevenson has painted and link these words of yesterday to your world of tomorrow, your master plan.

ACHIEVEMENT:

That man is a success who has lived well, laughed often and loved much; who has gained the respect of intelligent men and the love of children; who has filled his niche and accomplished his task; who leaves the world better than he found it, whether by improved poppy, a perfect poem or a rescued soul; who never lacked appreciation of the earth's beauty or failed to express it; who looked for the best in others and gave the best he had.

—Robert Louis Stevenson

You might have noticed that this verse uses only the male gender. Not to worry—Stevenson wasn't a chauvinist, he was simply using the vernacular of the era. This piece was written long before the women's rights movement; consider "man" synonymous with all people.

NONLINKED DECISIONS

I recently had a man visit my office who couldn't stop talking about what a success he was. You know the type, an obnoxious braggart, listing all of his accomplishments, boasting about his lifestyle, and the money he earned. I don't know about you, but this type of person gets on my nerves, even in my counseling practice. Anyway, when he stopped to catch his breath from all his bragging, I asked him to talk about the purpose of his visit. It was as if I had opened the floodgates. Suddenly this man, who I'll refer to as Bill, talked about his failed marriage, his children who he never visited, recurring headaches, excessive drinking, a bad temper, and his obvious obesity problem.

You could glance at Bill and see that he is a living time bomb, an accident waiting to happen. It certainly doesn't take a trained counselor to figure this out. Poor Bill never operated from a master plan. He made isolated decisions that were linked to nothing but his immediate needs—be it ego, money, status, or recognition. Now his life is a disaster. Sure he makes good money, but the ringing of his cash register has a hollow sound to it.

Would you model yourself after Bill? Does he personify your definition of high achievement? I hope not! Go review our academic research project of high achievers and you'll see that Bill is not even close. Such is the result of isolated decisions that are not linked to a master plan.

Another story is far more tragic. Herbie, a talented 20-year-old, got married while in college and then dropped out to start a business. He had earned his tuition by driving a moving truck, recognized the potential, and decided to compete with his former boss.

An ambitious plan, yes. But Herbie was involved with drugs, both using and selling, and they would eventually take his life. The real reason he dropped out of college was because of poor grades—it's hard to study when taking drugs—and he married his high school sweetheart as a crutch. She was pretty, bright, and her family had enough money to help get the business off the ground. But Herbie's untimely death from a drug overdose soon after his marriage was not a total surprise to those who really knew him. His life was a continuous stream of non-linked decisions that focused on immediate gratification.

Although the cause of this tragedy appears obvious in hindsight, it is actually a series of isolated decisions that were not linked to a master plan. Whether it was the drugs, dropping out of school, or getting married, all were serious decisions made without any regard to the future. Although the details vary, there are thousands of young Herbies. Whether it's hanging with the wrong crowd, trying too hard to be cool, doing drugs, carrying guns, committing random acts of violence, or simply neglecting schoolwork—you probably know people like this. Avoid them like the plague!

PUTTING EVERYTHING INTO PERSPECTIVE

Life is far too short, much too fragile, and too much fun not to be enjoyed at every step throughout your journey. You must have fun! This must be part of your plan. And the good news is that **fun** doesn't put you at risk with your future. Therefore your Master Dream List should actually be a plan. And it must include balance! Paying attention to your health doesn't mean you can never eat another hamburger. Living with sound spiritual values doesn't require you to go into the ministry and save the world. Being a responsible, loving, and caring family member does not eliminate friends outside of the family. Getting good grades and studying hard does not make you a square.

I know this might seem a bit heavy at first, but this is what you can control: not how long you are going to live, but how long you would like to live, and what would you like to accomplish during your journey through life. Most people, especially young adults, can't think beyond the upcoming year, much less map out their dreams or determine how long they would like to live—which is why most people have little control over their lives, continue to make unlinked decisions, and remain unfulfilled. Actually, this is an exercise in cause and effect. Few people dying of lung cancer planned such a painful death. Likewise, Herbie did not plan to fall into the drug trap—he simply did not have a long-range plan. It's that simple.

This is why only after you project how long you would like to live should you determine what you would like to accomplish during your lifetime and the lifestyle you would like to create. Do you want a family? What type of career interests you? Where would you like to live? Would you like to travel? What income would you desire? What are the opportunities to which you can apply your talents? What type of relationship do you want to have with your parents, brothers, sisters, and in-laws? How would you like to be remembered?

Okay. Enough of that, I know. It's extremely difficult for anyone to think that far into the future. Yet Mickey Mantle, one of baseball's true legends, suffered a sad and painful death from a lifetime of alcohol abuse and this is a vivid reminder of the perils of not working from a master plan with balance. Only after it was too late did the Mick recognize the error of his ways. Sadly, like many less recognizable faces, he departed before his time because he never linked his activities of today to a master plan for tomorrow.

However, those people who can plan their future are able to live a life that is the envy of others. Don't rush as you work through this exercise in your notebook. The time is now to begin mapping out your future. Your Master Dream List is a perfect starting point. Years ago, a 15-year-old named John Goddard proved this to the adult world.

In the next chapter I am going to show you how to link your dreams to immediate objectives that are important to you right now, and develop a specific action plan that will ensure your dreams do become a reality.

WRAP-UP

- Dream your future.
- Be specific in your dreams.
- Revisit John Goddard's Master Dream List.
- Create your own Master Dream List using the four categories: professional, personal, family, and spiritual.
- How long would you like to live?
- Think first things first.
- Link all decisions to your plan, your Master Dream List.
- Plan to enjoy every stage of your life!

Chapter 6

Activity Drives the Master Dream List

"Genius is one percent inspiration and ninety-nine percent perspiration."

—Thomas Alva Edison

By progressing this far, you have already taken major strides in harnessing the power of your mind to work constructively for you. You have laid the foundation upon which you can build your life. You are in control of the programming powers of your mind, a Master Dream List has focused your attention on the future, and now you are ready to act—to link everything from this point forward to your most immediate objective. First things first. This is where the rubber meets the road.

Everyone dreams, especially young adults, but very few are able to transform their dreams into reality. Undoubtedly you know some people thus afflicted. Oh, there are many reasons—excuses, to be more exact. But it has been my experience that the major obstacle that keeps people with the best of intentions from gaining control over their lives is inactivity. They fail to Do—those necessary activities linked to their dreams.

Talk is cheap. Agreed? But how many people do you know who talk a good game yet never seem capable of putting it all together? Quite a few, I'm sure. You know, the friend who swears she's going to work harder this year, make the Dean's List and graduate with honors. Yet she remains a party animal with poor grades. The world is full of people like that. For some reason they are never able to act on their best intentions.

It's easy to get excited about creating a Master Dream List, anyone can do that. But unless there is immediate action directly linked to a specific dream, it's all is for nothing. You know what I'm talking about—the work part of the equation. Right? Everybody would love to have the lifestyle of their dreams but, hey, there's no free lunch. You have to pay the price. This is true in all aspects of life. And your price, like that of any achiever, is to act. It shouldn't be that difficult for people to figure out. But it is. . . .

Take Sally for example. In her mid-thirties, Sally was a working mother of three. She was a customer service representative. Never able to regain her shape after the birth of her third child, Sally had gained a considerable amount of weight. Convinced that her appearance was keeping her from getting a higher paying position in sales where she would have constant face-to-face interaction with the public, she came to my office to learn how to lose weight.

On the surface, it appeared everything was ready for success. Sally had a dream of becoming a sales rep, envisioned how the additional income would impact her family, and had linked losing weight as the first step. She began our initial session by stating her dreams, ''I need to lose weight in order to be considered for a sales position in my company. That would double my income and enable us to move into a larger house, in a better neighborhood, with better schools. So I've got to lose this weight!''

I don't know about you, but Sally certainly sounded as though she had given a good deal of thought to her plan. She had a dream that was linked to specific accomplishments (sales position and weight loss), which required her immediate action. First things first.

She agreed to a simple approach to losing weight that had been extremely successful with other people—modeling both the attitude and behavior of healthy and fit people. More specifically, she was to eat three balanced meals per day, avoiding desserts, fried foods, and junk food. The other half of her health and fitness equation centered around exercise; she was to walk briskly for 30 to 45 minutes every morning. She was to record her affirmation tape, listen to it daily, and affirm constantly to herself, "I'm healthy and fit, I like myself!" There were to be no diet plans, no real restriction, no demeaning weigh-in sessions, as negativity was to be avoided at all costs. She had to stop worrying about her weight and start acting like a healthy, fit person.

But dreaming, and acting on your dreams, are two entirely different propositions. Sally was able to talk a good dream. She had even created an action plan. But upon returning to my office two weeks later, all I heard were excuses: "My job is driving me crazy! We had a quality-control problem that required a lot of customer service attention. It forced me to work through lunch, stay late, and basically threw my entire planned schedule out of whack. Could we start all over?" she asked apologetically.

Of course Sally could start over. But that was not her problem. It was an inability to act on her dreams. Oh, she could articulate them well enough, but for some reason she couldn't seem to adjust her routine to make anything happen. I had counseled her about all the needed changes—going to bed earlier in order to walk in the morning, bringing lunch and eating at her desk, preparing meals for the week on the weekend, and bringing fruit to work as a precaution against eating inappropriate foods when working late.

Her response was a simple, "Oh, you make it sound so simple." Well, you decide. Is it? Simple only if you are committed to your dreams and willing to act accord-

ingly. Sally visited my office one more time and was doing better. But she still wasn't walking every day and was
skipping lunch on occasion. I wish I could tell you that
her dreams were realized, but at this writing she is still
working at trying to do all of her specific fixed daily activities.

Have you ever fallen into the trap that Sally's trying to
pull out of? Most people have. Part of Sally's challenge,
which is symptomatic of many adults, is that she has created so many bad habits that she is beginning to believe
her own excuses—which is the ultimate trap. Rarely is a
student as mired in so many bad habits.

Best intentions and 25 cents might get you a soft drink
at Wal-Mart. But only specific activity linked to a dream,
a target, will bring about a positive result.

FIRST THINGS FIRST: PRIORITIZING YOUR PLAN

It's time to sit down in a quiet spot and reflect on your
Master Dream List. Which dreams are most immediate?
For students this usually involves some aspect of school-
ing, whether it is graduating from high school with the
grades necessary for acceptance into the college of choice,
or an SAT score, or grades in college, night school, trade
school, etc. But you also need to focus on you at this
stage in your life, so let's focus on both professional
(school) and personal categories and develop immediate
targets that are linked to your Master Dream List. Immediate targets that will force you to act **now**!

In your Mind Power Notebook, directly following the
section you have set aside for your Master Dream list,
label two facing pages ''Immediate School Accomplishments'' and ''Immediate Personal Accomplishments,'' re-
spectively. We're shifting gears now, leaving the world
of dreams and moving into the world of the immediate.

Don't worry if you haven't completed your Master Dream List; some of you have yet to really get started with it, I know. But at least you're thinking about it, which is the first step in linking your immediate concerns to your future.

As I have mentioned before, your school accomplishments will probably revolve around grades. Your personal accomplishments might involve sports, scouts, a musical instrument, a trip to Europe, or even a heart-throbbing crush on someone. All that matters is its importance to you.

Once you have established two top-priority accomplishments that are of immediate importance, it's time to create specific action plans that will lead you to these accomplishments. I generally refer to these action plans as "Fixed Daily Activities." Why? Because I want you thinking in terms of developing a daily routine, which will naturally evolve into a powerful positive habit. Not simply your current action plan, but the habit of being involved with fixed daily activities that are linked to your upcoming dream (accomplishment).

Activity Association Question: What three activities could you do (that you're currently not doing, or are doing poorly) that are totally in your control and would enable you to achieve your most immediate accomplishments? This will become your fixed daily activity list. It will drive you to those immediate accomplishments to which they are linked. For instance, your school fixed daily activity list might look something like this:

1. Two hours of studying after school in the library
2. Thirty minutes per night, per course, of pretest preparation
3. Two hours per day, Saturday and Sunday, spent on schoolwork

Everyone must create their own fixed daily activities, I
simply wanted to give you a model that can guide you.
Notice how each activity is completely within the control
of the person making the commitment. It's like the case
of Sally taking her 30-minute brisk walk: either it's done,
or it's not. Regardless, it's up to Sally to make the walk
happen. It's not up to her how fast she loses weight, but
rather the fixed daily activities that are linked to that objective are in her control. The same holds true for you.

Later in the chapter you will find a Fixed Daily Activity
Commitment. Until then, write down various activities
that come to mind as you continue reading. Basically, I
am asking you to break your Master Dream List down to
the lowest common denominator. You have to exercise
your conscious mind to determine what activities are necessary to turn your immediate dreams into reality. This
becomes a Mind Power exercise and internal management
challenge, a discipline. In most instances, the fixed daily
activities driving your dreams are not glamorous. They
are hard work!

For example, Billy dreams of being a foreign diplomat.
He longs to travel the world and experience other cultures.
But first he must get into NYU, as it has one of the better
graduate programs in this particular field. A high SAT
score is required, in addition to top grades in every course.
Billy's fixed daily activities involved taking an SAT preparation course, and spending one hour a day on SAT preparation. He was excelling in all subjects except math, so
he determined to spend two hours per week with a math
tutor and spend an extra 45 minutes per day studying
math. Since he loved history, Billy also decided to begin
a self-study program, which involved reading for a minimum of 30 minutes every day from some book dealing
with ancient history. Sounds like work, doesn't it? Not
really. Because Billy is fully engaged in becoming a foreign correspondent, the only real work is the extra time

he is committing to math and the SAT. Otherwise he is simply putting daily discipline to what he is already doing.

PUTTING IT ALL INTO PERSPECTIVE

My first exposure to the real challenges facing students was as a young therapist in Greensboro, North Carolina. I had just moved from Worcester, Massachusetts, and was actively working at making a name for my counseling practice. Using therapeutic hypnosis as a primary modality set me apart from the other counselors. This was back in the days when there was very little public awareness about hypnosis outside of the stage-show stereotype, much less any understanding of its therapeutic value.

Because of my atypical background, an MBA in marketing coupled with therapeutic hypnosis counseling, I was frequently asked to speak to local civic organizations. Although I wasn't a trained public speaker, I forced myself to accept every offer to speak, my local exposure quickly grew, and soon clients were visiting my office from all parts of North and South Carolina. Becky De-Haven was one of these early clients. She taught at a local college and was in the midst of organizing an SAT preparation course. She asked if I would conduct a session on studying and testing. She was convinced that most students used their Mind Power destructively during big tests and the SAT simply exacerbated this. Because of Becky's enthusiasm and encouragement, I agreed.

Becky was right. She had warned me these students were a bundle of nerves when it came to tests, and that the magnitude of the SAT simply added fuel to an already bad case of nerves. My task was simple and twofold: first, to teach them how to relax and study, and then how to relax and test. What I didn't anticipate was such a complete lack of goal focus. Nobody was working from a plan. Only one student had determined what score he needed to get into the college of his, or his parents', choice.

So here I was confronted with 25 students, using their Mind Power destructively through worry, who didn't have a clue as to how this SAT test linked to their future. All they knew was that parents and teachers seemed to place their entire future on this silly test. The message was clear: They had better do well.

Amazingly, my job became very simple: put first things first. I explained how the mind worked and gave them a simple goal exercise to assist them in using their Mind Power constructively. And guess what? That goal exercise just happened to involve a specific SAT score linked to a college. Next I taught a simple self-hypnosis, relaxation-visualization technique to be used every day before studying and prior to any test, not just the SAT. I coupled this with a mental signal to stimulate concentration while studying and memory recall while testing. (You will learn these techniques in a later chapter.)

Their studying routine now changed from simply studying when the mood hit to using goal-focused self-hypnosis and mental signaling. My selling point to them was explaining how this technique would probably eliminate 40 percent of their study time due to their improved powers of concentration and memory recall, resulting from practicing self-hypnosis and using their mental signals.

Imagine these kids telling their parents that the SAT preparation course recommended they spend less time studying! Much less time, and replace some of it with a few minutes of self-hypnosis. Yeah, right! But these students did my suggested fixed daily activities and the average scores increased over 100 points! But the point I want to make is about control.

FOCUS ON WHAT YOU CAN CONTROL

Rather than worry about where business was going to come from, how I was going to develop a reputation and attract clients to my practice, I acted. By speaking in front of various civic groups, not only did I increase my exposure but I also boosted my confidence. I was learning how to handle an audience, think on my feet, and speak in public. Many therapists with far more experience avoided public speaking. Their loss, my gain. Why? Because I acted and they did not. Therefore I grew while they kept doing the same old routine. Yet I am certain they would have liked to expand their counseling practices.

No matter how desperately you want to get a good grade, or become an all-county baseball player, or whatever the accomplishment, if you allow your mind to be consumed with things over which you do not have the ability to exert absolute control—you're stuffed! Often this takes the form of worry. Worrying about such things as the difficulty of an upcoming test, a teacher being too strict, or the job market in the year 2000 is destructive. I might have worried about whether an audience would enjoy my speech or whether I would make a fool of myself. But these kinds of things are beyond our ability to control. Focusing on events outside our control is like turning the power switch in the mind to negative.

The trick is to do the activities you can control. Getting in motion, doing activities that are linked to one of your dreams, is probably the most effective way to turn the power switch in your mind to positive. Regardless of those areas of potential worry outside your control, by doing you gain freedom from such destructive forces. The fact is that most people, students included, focus far too much attention on areas they can't control, and spend too little time doing activities they can control. Get it?

In Chapter 11 I am going to take you, step by step, through what I refer to as the Achievement Cycle. You will have a thorough understanding of the importance of being engaged in activities that are directly linked to a goal, a dream, an immediate objective.

For now it is important to understand that there is no way you can control every one of the desired accomplishments on your Master Dream List. Sorry, but Mind Power has its limitations. But you can most definitely influence these accomplishments by disciplining yourself to do the fixed daily activities linked to your most immediate dreams. This is exactly what I was able to get these SAT students to do—shift their focus from events outside their control (the difficulty of the SAT, etc.), and get them to act on events they could control. Suddenly they were able to turn the power switches in their minds from negative to positive. It's no wonder they improved their scores.

TOO MANY PEOPLE HAVE THIS REVERSED

Heather, an attractive 15-year-old high school sophomore, had her power switch locked on negative. She had been constantly putting much too much pressure on herself by focusing on events outside her control. Much of this wasn't her fault. Her mother was a source of constant pressure, which had intensified when her father had walked out three years earlier. Now her school grades were suffering and Heather had developed a nervous habit of pulling her hair.

Not only did Heather pull her hair, she was pulling it out of her head! By the time she visited my office she was wearing an unattractive wig and couldn't look anyone in the eye. What happened following the destruction of her family unit? Heather began to blame herself for her father's departure. If only she had been a better daughter, if only she was prettier, if only she had made the soccer team, and so on, as her mind was quietly taking her down the path of destruction.

She probably would have worked through this over time with counseling if her mother had left her alone. But her mother did the opposite. She transferred all of her attention to Heather, basically transferring her hurt and worry. So now destructive energy was everywhere and neither mother nor daughter were focused on the future. There was no plan, no Master Dream List, no plans for a future without a father in the picture.

That negative power switch often creates negative behavior that seems far removed from the picture. In Heather's case, whenever she attempted to study, her mind would drift off into worry and she would quietly pull at her hair. It wasn't long before her grades suffered, her hair loss became visible, and her mother started to panic. As difficult as it had become, neither Heather nor her mother were engaged in activities linked to a plan. Rather, they were focused on problems outside of their control.

But the hair pulling and poor grades were completely within Heather's control. After creating a specific action plan, linked to an immediate objective, a mini-dream, Heather's job was simply to do the fixed daily activities we had jointly created. Her goal was to get rid of the wig, and raise her grades to A's and B's. Part of her plan involved tactics for dealing with her mother, tactics for studying, and tactics to keep her from hair pulling. (Heather eliminated the basic hair-pulling habit through a session of therapeutic hypnosis.)

Not only did Heather succeed, she learned a valuable lesson that hopefully will remain with her throughout her life—to focus only on activities that she can control. She also learned to link activities, first things first, to dreams. In her case it was important to keep all of her dreams immediate because of the severity of her current problems. Her Master Dream List would come later.

IMPACT FACTORS, EXTERNAL AND INTERNAL

As Heather's case illustrates, events outside of your control will always impact your life. Although Heather's situation was extreme, things like weather, your brothers and sisters, your teachers and where you live, are more normal and still outside of your own control. Therefore, regardless of the impact they might have on your life, you don't want to waste time and energy worrying about them. As you know, worry becomes a habit for many people, and so does inactivity.

Whenever a student places blame for his lousy grades on a bad teacher, he is saying, "I can't be accountable for my performance." Failure is then rationalized, and this student becomes less effective learning the subject matter because now there is a built-in defense mechanism. This is typical whenever too much attention is given to external impact factors.

The basic law of the mind is: "You think it, you live it." Such is usually the case whenever a student is having trouble in school. Everyone knows someone who was always acting "cool," was often funny and getting into all kinds of minor trouble but was also always underachieving. You know the type, the student who never tries out for a sport, always gets poor grades, and is quick to make fun of anyone who is succeeding at anything. Unless the power switch is switched, a person like this goes through life controlled by external impact factors, and never gets anywhere near his or her potential.

Let's take a closer look at these impact factors. Internal impact factors are activities completely in your control—the fixed daily activities linked directly to your dreams. External impact factors are events outside of your control, like the difficulty of a particular test. When I refer to internal and external impact factors, I am always talking about events within or outside of your control.

Internal Impact Factors:	Specific activities that are completely in your control, fixed daily activities.
EXAMPLE:	Heather studying 45 minutes per subject, regardless of homework assignments.
External Impact Factors:	Anything that is out of your direct control.
EXAMPLE:	Heather's mother putting pressure on her.

There is so much blame being tossed around today that I often think many adults have made it an art form. Pick any issue, education, crime . . . the President blames the Senate, which blames the Congress, which blames Hollywood, or maybe it's the Senate that blames the President, who is blames both Hollywood and the Congress. Regardless of where the finger is being pointed and who is doing the pointing, little is being done. Rarely is any constructive action taken when people are ascribing blame.

Real achievers, the John Goddards of the world, do not point fingers. They act. Why? Because they take personal responsibility for their dreams. The power switch in such a person's mind is permanently in the positive position, and although external impact factors come and go, they never interfere.

This is important to understand, and because so few adults seem to have a clue I have compiled a partial list of some internal and external impact factors to assist you in this process. Go over this list and identify the external factors that have caused you problems in the past and determine to stop focusing on them. Also, you might find a couple of internal factors to add to your fixed daily activities. Understanding the difference will change your life!

IMPACT FACTORS

Internal	External
• Daily study time	• Difficulty of subject matter
• Master Dream List	• Date of accomplishments
• Daily exercise	• Your body type
• Eating three balanced meals	• Your exact weight daily
• Your communication with both your parents	• Your parents' communication with you
• Your positive attitude	• The attitude of other people
• Your fixed daily activities	• The actions of others

A brief glance at these comparisons provides most people with a working knowledge of where to focus their energy—on the internal impact factors, of course! Recognize the external impact factors that have caused you problems in the past, evaluate your previous responses, and then construct a plan of action that will help you work past future external impact factors, so you can concentrate on the internal factors. The idea is to focus only on what you can control!

TACTICS

Take Jimmy for example, the typical friend everyone has who works hard to be cool. He phones you constantly, always puts people down, and is a regular source of temptation—hang out rather than work out. We all have Jimmys in our lives, you know the type. This Jimmy, although lots of fun and a good friend, is not likely to be working from a Master Dream List. The odds are that he has no plan.

Yet the Jimmys in our lives can act as external impact factors. There is nothing you can do about their approach to life, other than be a good influence—which is precisely the tactic to take. First you must recognize your Jimmys, people of that nature, as external impact factors that could potentially interfere with your Master Dream List. Then you need to act accordingly: accept your Jimmys for who and what they are—they can be a lot of fun—and use their friendship as a recreational aspect of your life. Heck, they can help you stay balanced—as long as you remain linked to your Master Plan this potential external impact factor that could be a negative is suddenly transformed into a positive.

Your fixed daily activities will serve as your strategic commitment. Not only do they link you directly to your upcoming accomplishments (dreams), they protect you from those negative external impact factors. In essence, they guarantee your success. By the way, if your particular Jimmy refuses to allow you to use him as a positive force, if he openly attempts to derail you from following your Master Plan, you'd better start getting him out of your inner circle. He might not really be a true friend if he's going nowhere and trying to pull you along for the ride.

Your tactics for reaching your dreams, living up to your

wildest expectations, must center around what you can control. Arnold Schwarzenegger spent more time exercising both his body and mind than other bodybuilders. These activities were entirely within his control. He held himself accountable to maintain the discipline to **do** what was necessary, even when he didn't really want to exercise that particular day. You must do the same.

You have to hold yourself accountable for such discipline. Fixed daily activities require the discipline of doing them when you'd rather be doing something else. With that mind-set, then, and only then, will you have accepted the responsibility for actually working your Master Dream List.

ACTIVITY DRIVES THE DREAM

Okay, let's go back to the activity association question: What three activities have you selected (that you're currently not doing or that you are performing poorly) that are completely in your control and would play a major role in your most immediate dream? Keep in mind that you are applying the concept of linkage. These become your stepping-stones to your success journey through life. What activities must you attend to at this stage in your life, day after day, in order to achieve your most immediate goals?

There is no way around hard work and discipline. This is why most people overlook the critical aspect of achievement—doing. Few people are willing to pay the price. I know you see it every day. It's not cool to study. It's not cool to practice before and after practice. It's not cool to read. It's not cool to set goals for yourself. Right? Get real! Far too many students desperately want to control their lives, want the trappings of success, but aren't willing to do anything different to make it happen. The ultimate cool is being in control of your life, working from internal impact factors.

Your Master Dream List requires far more constructive behavior than many students possess, much less understand. You must make a commitment to this constructive behavior, fixed daily activities, far in advance of your accomplishments. This is the price you must pay for a wonderful life, and you must always pay in advance.

As you have probably gathered, your fixed daily activities are your workload. They must be challenging, more than simply doing your required homework, and you must become accustomed to paying in advance. You will be involved with some form of fixed daily activities at every stage of your life, as long you stay linked to your Master Dream List.

There's nothing easy about taking your time with homework, going over your classroom lessons, and spending a few minutes on additional study. There is nothing easy about getting up one hour earlier to exercise and get organized for your upcoming day. There is nothing easy about staying after wrestling practice to lift weights. There is also nothing easy about spending your adult life working at some dead-end job that you hate. Keep in mind that the people who get the best results are those who are willing to pay the price.

What's so interesting is the natural impact this has on that power switch in your mind. The more active you are working toward a goal, any goal, the easier it is to keep your Mind Power functioning constructively, the more true power you possess. The less active you are, the more you procrastinate, the more likely you are to have that power switch in your mind inadvertently stuck in the negative position, which is the ultimate sign of weakness.

With this in mind, I am going to challenge you to invest one full year to the Mind Power principles outlined in these chapters—one year of doing your fixed daily activities linked to your most immediate goal. After that time, you will be a living testimonial and hooked on these internal disciplines.

Now meet a couple of students I have worked with.

Professional (school):

Jennifer (16)—improve one grade in every subject

1. Do all homework before supper.
2. Spend between 15 to 30 minutes per course in additional study, after dinner.
3. Review daily class notes in afternoon study hall.

Martin (19)—make Dean's List

1. Transfer classroom notes to computer every day.
2. Attend every class and perform every assignment immediately.
3. Spend three hours in the library daily, four hours total on weekends.

Personal:

Jennifer (16)—backpack through southern France

1. Actively participate in the French club, speak French daily.
2. Baby-sit after school to earn money for the trip.
3. Research various hiking groups, and do something hiking-related daily.

Martin (19)—make the tennis team

1. Practice for one hour before classes.
2. Play at least one competitive set before dinner every day.
3. Spend 15 minutes daily working on serve

Naturally, these are the activities deemed important by Jennifer and Martin, but they might not make sense to anyone else. So be it. This is the nature of fixed daily activities. It's your dream, only you know what you are currently doing, and what could be done better.

Let's make your Fixed Daily Activity Commitment now. You can copy the Fixed Daily Activity Commitment form that follows on to a page in your Mind Power Notebook. It will become a very important reference point when you get into the chapter on synergistic goal getting.

FIXED DAILY ACTIVITY COMMITMENT   Date ___

In order to realistically achieve my most immediate professional/school dream (goal) of _____, I, _____, commit to holding myself daily accountable to the following three fixed daily activities:

1.
2.
3.

In order to realistically achieve my most immediate personal goal of _____, I, _____, commit to holding myself daily accountable to the following three fixed daily activities:

1.

2.

3.

Successful completion of these specific fixed daily activities is essential to my Master Dream List and gaining control of my life. I am accountable to myself for the daily performance of these specific activities.

Signature _____ Date_____

Because change is so difficult and your commitment to these fixed daily activities is so important, you will find the next chapter a little different. You are going to learn the importance of hooking up with another student and supporting each other in mastering Mind Power and taking control of your life. Let's face it, changing habits, both in your behavior and attitude, is much easier when you have the proper support. You are about to learn how to find such a supportive spirit.

WRAP-UP

- Spend time to accurately answer the Activity Association Question.
- Dreams without highly prioritized fixed daily activities are only "pipe dreams."
- Always concentrate your attention on what you can control—internal impact factors.

- Internal impact factors are those fixed daily activities linked to your most immediate dream (goal).
- You must make a commitment to doing your fixed daily activities.
- Reward yourself daily for doing your fixed daily activities.

Chapter 7

Your Dream Team Buddy: The Buddy System

"There is no such thing as a self-made man. You will reach your goals only with the help of others."

—George Shinn

You are about wean certain people from occupying any sort of influence in your life. Why? Because your journey is not going to include people who aren't willing to grow and take control over their lives. It's time for you to consider such people as a potential negative influence that could interfere with your plans. It's not that these people are bad and need to be eliminated from your life, but you must recognize them for what they are—if not, they can easily hold you back.

In guiding you through these chapters and explaining these timeless principles of Mind Power, I'm acting as your teacher, guide, and master coach. But, as you know, it's up to you to do it. It's at this point a Mind Power soul mate, a Dream Team Buddy, can be extremely helpful.

TWO HEADS ARE BETTER THAN ONE

Two heads are only better than one if they are supporting each other toward achieving a mutually agreed upon goal. Getting together with a friend to study for a big science test can be very useful as long as both of you are intent on getting the best possible grade on the science test. If one doesn't care, two heads are far worse than one.

As a high school and collegiate wrestler I always lifted weights. It took a lot of discipline and none of my team-mates had the same commitment. Although I went through many weight-lifting partners in high school, in college I found an ex-football player who had similar goals of increasing his strength. He became my weight-lifting partner and we dutifully met at the gym every day during our lunch period. In fact, we would arrange our classes around our lunch workouts. We both knew we would reach our strength goals faster if we encouraged, supported, and held each other accountable. I estimate our workouts were at least 25 percent better when we lifted together. We were soul mates.

Welcome to positive peer pressure. It is time to hook up with a friend who, like yourself, would like to take control of his/her life. You are embarking on a journey that is going to require discipline and focus. You must be accountable to both your dreams and those activities that will drive them. So why not a little support along the way?

THE MAGIC OF SHARING

Sharing your Master Dream List with a friend who is also interested in getting more out of life can be a magical experience. Sharing inner growth always brings out this kind of power. Whenever I conduct a workshop or give a lecture, I always ask the people in the audience to share something they've learned within 24 to 48 hours. This is for students and adults alike. The reason is simple. The value of the information strengthens considerably when the student becomes the teacher.

The impact is amazing. People pay closer attention, take better notes, and get more involved in the learning experience—all for the simple reason that they are planning to teach this material to someone else. It can be a parent, a younger brother, and older sister . . . it doesn't really matter. What is important is the strengthening of the commitment to learning.

If students and parents had the time to go over the day's lessons every evening, with the student teaching the parent, learning would accelerate. But we all know, for many varied reasons, that this will never happen. Likewise, learning is never as powerful when you are learning only from a book. It is for these reasons I have determined to present you with a working alternative.

THE BUDDY SYSTEM

Even in my workshops I go beyond simply asking people to teach what they have learned. After taking people through exercises that have enabled them to created fixed daily activities linked to a goal, I give a very specific homework assignment. Knowing that in many instances I will never see these people again, and that the best intentions are typically not enough to maintain the discipline necessary to change, I pair everyone with a partner. The idea is to connect two people with similar commitments to growth so they can support each other, hold each other accountable, and give honest feedback to one another.

SUPPORT GROUPS: ONE DAY AT A TIME

This isn't a new concept. People all over the world are discovering that by concentrating on what they can control, and through talking, listening, and sharing with their peers, long-term change can be accomplished. The power of the buddy system can be illustrated by the success of Alcoholics Anonymous.

Many years ago, in Toledo, Ohio, a stockbroker and a physician developed an historic buddy system to help keep them sober. Both were helpless drunks, no breakthrough discoveries were being made on the cause and cure of alcoholism, and these two professional men discovered the magic of both supporting and being accountable to each other.

Eventually this buddy system evolved into a program that is now the foundation of most support groups—the famous Twelve Steps. Regardless of the objective, be it sobriety or the Dean's List, having a kindred spirit assisting you in maintaining your daily disciplines is priceless—like the old saying about honesty, "The key to honesty is helping an honest person remain honest." Change "honesty" to "discipline" and you have the essence of what the buddy system can do for you. It's much like the motto of AA—"One day at a time." You can handle that. Your buddy can handle that. And together you will keep each other honest. Oops, I mean disciplined.

SELECTING YOUR BUDDY

Think of a friend you connect with on a deeper level. You know, a person you can really share your inner thoughts with and, rather than laugh at your wildest expectations, one who possesses the character to be able to quietly support you; a person who, deep inside, shares similar aspirations. Essentially, the buddy system requires two people who are willing to make an affirmation tape, create a Master Dream List, commit to fixed daily activities, and be held accountable for applying constructive Mind Power principles in every aspect of life. Your buddy will need to read this book, get involved with all the exercises, and be willing to grow. Understood?!

So do be careful in selecting your buddy. Think of it as selecting a partner in your journey of success. You definitely don't want a deadbeat! You must hook up with a fellow student who shares a similar desire to act on his/her dreams. If you select poorly, your buddy can pull you down. Negative peer pressure will surface as this person will attempt to steal your dreams by keeping you from doing your fixed daily activities. Why? Because unless a person is actively tracking a dream, he or she is uncomfortable with people who are. You know the old saying, "Misery loves company." Yet a well-chosen buddy will develop into a powerful alliance between peers. You each become an active member of the other's Dream Team. Hey, that has a nice ring to it. The buddy system is actually your Dream Team.

If it's easy for you to meet, I recommend meeting daily. You can study together, exercise together, and very effectively hold each other accountable for doing your fixed daily activities. At a minimum, schedule a Dream Team meeting once a week to discuss various Mind Power exercises and your Master Dream List, share experiences of the week, give each other feedback, and of course, hold each other accountable for staying on track with your Master Dream List.

You might be able to find a kindred spirit on-line. Somewhere on the Net there is a Dream Team Buddy waiting to assist you in living up to your wildest expectations. If you use technology to communicate with your buddy, make certain you transfer the appropriate Mind

Power Notebook exercises onto your computer. Everything from your Master Dream List and fixed daily activities to the affirmations on your 7-7-7 Tape.

Technology aside, keep in mind that the idea of peers supporting peers is not a new achievement concept. Thomas Edison, the father of the light bulb, had less than three months of formal education when in 1876 he created his dream team in the form of a Master Mind Alliance. The idea was to pool the talents of various engineers, model makers, scientists, mathematicians, and skilled mechanics. Sixty-one people, all committed to growth and to help each other grow. Their goal was to have a minor invention every 10 days and a major invention every six months. In less than six years, Edison alone held more than 300 patents! Dream teams are timeless.

PLEASE NOTE: You can make magic out of this book without a Dream Team Buddy. There is tremendous value to finding someone who can read, discuss, and go through all the exercises with you. If you can find such a buddy, each of you should have your own copy so you can establish regular reading assignments and meetings. You will share and accelerate your growth. Think of the buddy system as your Dream Team.

FEEDBACK—ACCOUNTABILITY—SUPPORT

The objective of having a Dream Team Buddy is to develop a relationship that goes far beyond petty jealousies. You are living the old proverb, ''The more you help someone else achieve their goals, the closer you come to realizing your goals.''

Before selecting your Dream Team Buddy, you might

find it useful to have this person complete the following Feedback, Accountability, Support Profile. If everything seems to make sense to both of you, establish a timetable for collectively going through the chapters up to this point. You will need to bring your new buddy up to speed. Share your affirmation tape, your Master Dream List, and fixed daily activities. Let me first define what I mean by feedback, accountability, and support.

Feedback:	Think in terms of constructive advice. Most people are quick to criticize, but seldom offer any useful suggestions for overcoming a particular obstacle. Criticism kills dreams. Feedback enables you to deftly hurdle the challenges along the way. You both must allow feedback without becoming defensive. Make certain a discussion follows all feedback.
Accountability:	The objective of a Dream Team Buddy is to make certain both of you achieve your dreams. Therefore everyone on the team must allow the others to hold them accountable for doing their fixed daily activities linked to their most immediate dream. This is not just a bull session. Sure you can have fun, talk sports, girls, boys, and so on. But limit this idle chatter. If your buddy hasn't spent the appropriate time in the library, exercise room, or whatever the fixed daily activity might be, you must let it be known that such ne-

glect is unacceptable. Everyone needs an occasional nudge, and we must be willing to accept it. Are you ready? This is very strategic peer pressure.

Support: Nothing is more important in making your Dream Team effective than a genuine interest and concern for the successes and challenges facing your buddy. Too many people go through life too self-serving. You know the ME, ME, ME mentality. Not you. You are going to be involved in a true "win-win" situation.

FASP: FEEDBACK, ACCOUNTABILITY, SUPPORT PROFILE

Instructions: This profile is designed to help you differentiate between criticism and feedback, friendship and support, accountability and excuses. You need to be fully aware of your past tendencies. For best results, answer each question honestly.

	Strongly Agree	Mildly Agree	Mildly Disagree	Strongly Disagree
1. I don't like people questioning my actions.	4	3	2	1
2. I resent people giving me advice.	4	3	2	1

3. I resent students who appear to be high achievers. 4 3 2 1

4. I am very concerned with what other people think of me. 4 3 2 1

5. I often make excuses for not doing what I intended. 4 3 2 1

6. I can be highly critical of others. 4 3 2 1

7. My friends are terrific and support my goals. 1 2 3 4

8. I don't allow people to know the real me. 4 3 2 1

9. I look for the best in others. 1 2 3 4

10. I am honest with myself. 1 2 3 4

Scoring the FASP: You will determine your FASP score by adding the number circled.

Maximum Score = 40   My Score _____

40–36	You've got to pay close attention to making your Dream Team Buddy relationship an effective one. Relax. This is a new concept for most.
35–29	You've got some feel for feedback, accountability, and support. But now is the time for application!
28–21	Average. You are influenced both positively and negatively by your peers.
20–14	Without realizing it, or perhaps you do realize it, you are already benefiting from your peers.
13 and below	Keep doing more of what you're doing. Great!

Areas for Improvement: Review the individual items on the Profile and determine specific areas that you need to develop, strengthen, and enhance in your efforts to stay committed to your dreams. If you have:

Circled 4, you've identified an area to Develop.
Circled 3, you've identified an area to Strengthen.
Circled 2, you've identified an area to Capitalize upon.

Select three areas that you are going to work on now. List them in your Mind Power Notebook under "FASP Areas to Improve" and create a simple action plan for correcting each area. If you have a buddy, discuss the areas you've both selected and help each other carry out your respective action plans.

LOOKING CLOSELY IN THE MIRROR

As you begin looking for a buddy, it's a good idea to take
a long look in the mirror. No, you're not looking for zits,
rather you are trying to identify true strengths and weaknesses. Where do you excel? Are you disciplined? Do you
find yourself easily influenced by others? Basically you
are looking to determine what barriers, if any, you per-
ceive that could keep you from your Master Dream List.
Is there anything holding you back?

The following list is merely a guide. You can expand
on it as you like as you rate each item either a strength
or a weakness in your Mind Power Notebook.

                              STRENGTHS   WEAKNESSES

Discipline
Achievement Drive
Attitude
Health
Study Habits
Concentration
Energy
Communication
Persistence
Humor
Fitness
Decision-making
Goal Orientation
Work Habits
Honesty
Family Focus
Values
Positive Role Model

YOUR DREAM TEAM BUDDY AGREEMENT

I, _____ , am accountable to correct:

_____

_____

I accept feedback to help me develop:

_____

_____

I welcome support and accountability to capitalize on:

_____

_____

Signature_____ Date_____

Signature_____ Date_____

Taken seriously, this document is very important to your personal growth. Keep it where you can refer to it frequently and adjust it at your weekly meetings. As soon as you find a Dream Team Buddy, go over this agreement together. Not only is your buddy going to help you stay focused on your dreams, but this is a special person who can provide constructive insight to various strengths and weaknesses that you might have overlooked. After all, we all have blind spots.

So many of nature's gifts are overlooked. Learning how to relax and win is one of the most frequently overlooked gifts. Stress seems to have gained the upper hand.

Whether it's you preparing for a test, or your parents rushing to work, few people understand the secret of staying relaxed under pressure. Those who do, usually win.

In the next chapter, I'm going to teach you how to relax and absorb knowledge while studying, how to relax and stimulate free-flowing memory recall when testing, and how to use this powerful tool in every area of your life. It's the ultimate in Mind Power. Keep reading.

WRAP-UP

- Find a Dream Team Buddy, someone who is willing to grow with you.
- A good buddy will accelerate your growth and mastery of Mind Power.
- Feedback, support, and accountability are essential to an effective buddy relationship.
- Recognize your strengths and weaknesses.
- Commit to your buddy.

Chapter 8

How to Relax and Win

"The two words, 'peace' and 'tranquility,' are worth a thousand pieces of gold."
— Chinese proverb

Now that you've created your self-programming cassette tape, are developing a Master Dream List, have linked specific fixed daily activities to immediate objectives, and have found a Dream Team Buddy to assist you in driving your dreams, allow me to introduce you to one of nature's key components to Mind Power—**relaxation**. Most of you will understand the following message, probably much better than either of your parents. . . .

One of the most productive activities you can do that will benefit every aspect of your life—accelerate learning, build confidence, maintain a positive attitude, and perform well under pressure—is to learn how to relax. And it's actually easier than most people think.

I will never forget Marcia. Working as a salesperson at an advertising agency, she had graduated from law school and had flunked the bar exam twice, which is the test every graduating law student is required to pass before they can begin practicing law. Needless to say, it's a high-pressure test. Marcia's last attempt left her so devastated that she had given up the thought of ever becoming a lawyer. It had been five years since her last attempt. One of her dreams was fading away, unachieved.

Life is full of crazy coincidences, and of all places I

might have met Marcia it was on the tennis court that our paths crossed. A mutual friend introduced us, embarrassing Marcia by briefly explaining her plight and suggesting I might be of some assistance. It was obvious to Bob, our mutual friend, that Marcia had been so beaten down by this bar exam problem that, left alone, she would never muster up the courage to address it.

A few days later as Marcia sat in my office, it was painful to listen to her describe how she failed the second time. "I'm not a stupid person," she explained. "I graduated from law school. But I always got nervous taking tests. And the more important the test, the more nervous I would get. I thought I would pass the first time, but I got too nervous. But the second time was a joke. I couldn't sleep, I couldn't study, all I could think about was 'What if I flunked again? I'd have wasted all that money going to law school.' It was the most painful experience in my life!"

Marcia is now a practicing attorney. After only two visits to my office she learned how to use relaxation techniques to access Mind Power for both studying and taking the bar exam. She learned how to visualize herself taking the exam and passing. She practiced her relaxation technique before every study session. This technique became one of her fixed daily activities. Incidentally, she estimated that she spent 50 percent less time studying.

"Nothing can bring you peace but yourself."
—Ralph Waldo Emerson

You don't need me to remind you that students have become so stressed out with tests that often they do the opposite of what is necessary, and this prevents them from accessing constructive Mind Power. They try to meet every test by studying harder, spending more hours in front of their books, and worrying more. Wrong! The answer is in studying smarter, using your time efficiently and not worrying at all. So much precious studying time is wasted when the mind is consumed with worry. Worry is negative, lowers the concentration to a level too low for absorbing knowledge effectively, and little is accomplished other than increasing the level of frustration. You feel like you're spinning your wheels. Has this ever happened to you?

In today's high-stress world a quick glance at most adults will validate the importance of being able to relax. Most adults have a big problem in this area. Surprisingly—or perhaps it's not so surprising—more and more students are being overwhelmed with the pressures associated with formal education. You know the routine: "If you don't get A's and B's you'll never amount to anything! Look at Mark, the boy down the street, he gets all A's and he's in the accelerated program." You've probably heard your version of this parental comparison game. It makes your stomach churn, I know.

Relax. Think of it as just another example of adult stress-out. Nothing is that life threatening to worry about or lose any sleep over. You have already learned how to program your mind through affirmations. Simply telling yourself, "I'm relaxed and confident," will, if repeated enough, help bring on that desired result. This chapter is going to take your reprogramming one step further through the strategic use of relaxation. Derived from therapeutic hypnosis and autohypnosis, I refer to it as "suggestive relaxation."

Whether you are climbing Mt. Everest like John Goddard, shooting foul shots like Michael Jordan, studying for a final exam, or going on your first date, this technique will serve as the foundation of all your Mind Power resources. It will enable you to incorporate all these Mind Power exercises into every aspect of your life. Some of these exercises you have yet to learn. Your ability to relax is essential for the synergistic goal-getting exercise in the

next chapter. You will learn how to bring your Master
Dream List to life through relaxation and sensory-rich imagery. Being able to relax under pressure is critical to
success.

A FUNDAMENTAL LAW OF NATURE

Everybody is vulnerable. No person is immune. That's
something we all have to come to grips with at various
times in our lives. Every time you listen to one of your
parents overreact, a teacher yell at her class, or a friend
lose his cool you're witnessing people falling victim to
stress. It's destructive mind power.

Hey, it happens to the best of us. I can recall an embarrassing moment when I let stress get the best of me.
It was a Saturday and we, the entire family, had taken a
drive to the Blue Ridge Mountains of North Carolina. A
good friend was building a second home and were going
to spend a leisurely day in the mountains. Much of the
trip involved the possibility of my finding a remote spot
where we could, of all things, relax as a family.

All went well, the kids enjoyed the day, and we headed
back home to Greensboro. Within short order my wife
asked me why I was driving so fast. My response was
denial. Yet I realized I was rushing home to play tennis
with a neighbor. Well, no more thought was given to my
state of mind until we were in Greensboro and rushing to
rent a video for the kids. As circumstances outside my
control dictated, I found myself challenged with an over-
full parking lot with cars circling like vultures in hopes
of pouncing on an empty spot. I spotted a couple walking
to their car and followed them in anticipation of getting
their parking spot.

They got into their automobile but were in no hurry to
depart as they sat talking. Well, you might have guessed
what was happening to me. The stress buildup my wife

had noticed two hours earlier erupted and I suddenly honked the horn in frustration. The next thing I knew, both my wife and the lady in the parked car were lecturing me on my manners. A stress attack had raised its ugly head, destructive mind power surfaced and took a huge bite out of my state of mind. Not only did I feel lower than low for acting like an idiot, I knew better. Hey, was the speed in which this couple departed within my control? Yeah, right!

You guessed it, I played a lousy game of tennis. I got what I deserved, but the real issue was allowing myself to get so uptight. There was no way I could enjoy playing tennis, much less play very well. My point is simple; everyone needs to practice some form of relaxation technique constantly. Myself included. We all need to release the toxins in our system. Thus the importance of ''suggestive relaxation''—which can actually be considered a fixed daily activity that complements all others.

You might find it useful read some of the feedback I've received from students, of all ages, who have mastered the art of suggestive relaxation:

- ''It allows me to free myself from all of my pressures and visit my dreams.''
- ''My concentration while studying has improved 300 percent!''
- ''It helps me get to sleep at night.''
- ''I'm amazed how I am able to stay relaxed during tests, and how much that has helped my grades. I no longer choke.''
- ''My parents no longer get on my nerves like they used to.''
- ''I feel better about myself.''
- ''My headaches have gone away. I can't believe it!''
- ''It has lifted my tennis game to a new level.''

This is not idle praise. I could go on and on, as the rewards are endless. Learning how to relax is one of the most important aspects of developing a lifestyle for a lifetime of health and fitness. It is also one of the most overlooked. Too many adults feel they don't have the time to practice "suggestive relaxation." This is ironic, because these are always the same people who need it most.

RELAXATION AND SUBCONSCIOUS COMMUNICATION

People are amazed whenever I explain the impact relaxation has on our internal channels of communication. The fact is that your subconscious mind is much more receptive to suggestion when you are relaxed. In other words, your mind is more open to programming, which is why advertisements on television are so powerful. Whenever you watch television, your conscious mind becomes relaxed. You don't have to think. Your imagination, however, becomes fully activated. It plays along with whatever you happen to be watching. In this highly responsive mode you are then zapped with a commercial telling you some particular soft drink will make you hip, a particular sneaker will make you a better athlete, and so on.

You, as a student of mind power, can not take this power lightly. The fact is television advertising, along with the programs they sponsor, have a strong impact on people who spend hours glued to their televisions. Of course this isn't a new development. The Federal Communications Commission banned cigarette advertising from television long ago, while continuing to allow tobacco companies to use print media. The FCC recognized that the programming message urging people to smoke was too powerful with a relaxed conscious mind.

When your conscious mind is relaxed, your subconscious takes a much more active role in all forms of communication, leaving you much more vulnerable to suggestion. Think about those ads that hook you. Whether it's a beauty product, basketball shoes, fast food, or a car—these messages are targeted at you. Use this shampoo and be sexy, attract the girl, or boy, wear this basketball shoe and be cool, eat this food and be happy, drive this car and be smart . . . and the list is endless.

Big bucks are involved with this form of programming. You, my friend, will never be as vulnerable as the average viewer. Why? Because you are in control of your Mind Power, and most people aren't.

CONTROLLING THIS POWER

Nothing is magical about relaxation. It is one of those natural human functions everyone is capable of enjoying at all stages of life. Relaxation has been endowed to all of us at birth. If you're like many people, you are probably a bit rusty at the art of relaxation. It's nothing a little practice won't cure. Actually, it's quite easy.

Now if you're making the mistake thinking the relaxation I'm referring to is "vegging out" in your favorite chair watching MTV, think again. The relaxation you are about to master is a deep state of muscle relaxation. When this occurs, your pulse rate and blood pressure decrease, and your breathing becomes slower and more regular— all of which are extremely healthy, calming, psychological responses. Investing a mere 20 to 30 minutes a day in this type of relaxation can make all the difference to the quality of your life. Imagine being able to relax, on call, under extreme pressure. You will also be able to combine your time relaxing with your Mind Power goal-getting exercise, which you will learn in the next chapter.

The biggest problem people encounter in trying to master relaxation techniques—be it meditation, yoga, or self-hypnosis—is that they look for immediate results and therefore do not practice the technique for a long enough period of time. Patience, patience. This is the same reason so few people actively get the goals they set for themselves. Yet I have experienced tremendous success teaching suggestive relaxation, especially with students. Why? Because suggestive relaxation takes little time, involves goal-getting, and requires very little instruction. It's simple!

LINKING RELAXATION AND TENSION

Early in the twentieth century, Dr. Edmund Jacobsen concocted a method of relaxation that required some 200-odd exercises. Talk about simplicity—it's no wonder his methods never caught on. Regardless, his work was extremely important. Dr. Jacobsen was a lone voice in the Western world, helping people understand the relationship between relaxation and tension. As simple as it might seem today, Dr. Jacobsen was one of the first people in the West to recognize the importance of both states—that paradox between the natural tension associated with a major exam, and the necessity of being able to relax in order to score well. Sound crazy? Let's give it a go.

TENSION VERSUS RELAXATION EXERCISE

Consider the following two scenarios. Provide as much detail as possible.

- Think of something during the past 48 hours that caused pressure, made you nervous, tense, uptight, worried—a school project, a test, being called upon in class, a family problem, etc.

- Now recall an .event, other than sleep or television, that helped you feel relaxed.

What usually happens to the students in my workshops is that they find it easy to recall a stressful situation, and usually they can list more than one. But when it comes to relaxation, they struggle. Some have athletic coaches who have begun to incorporate relaxation exercises as a regular part of their practice sessions, but not many. As a rule, most students do not engage in regular relaxation exercises. Rather, they struggle with stress and the accompanying pressures.

AN HISTORICAL OVERVIEW OF RELAXATION

The Eastern world is built on the foundation of relaxation—peace of mind and body. All the Eastern cultures, differing in religion, customs, and politics, have common ground in their focus on the art of relaxation. Question: What do Indian yogis, martial arts masters, monks, and samurai warriors have in common? Answer: A working knowledge that a mind which can relax the body is a mind which can keep both mind and body strong.

Even though it has been years since Dr. Jacobsen and his associates worked diligently to assist people in understanding the relationship between relaxation and stress-related health problems, too many people in the Western world still haven't gotten the message. Rather than continually getting stressed out, you and other students should be learning relaxation techniques as a required part of your lessons. So much for wishful thinking. Could you imagine what your parents would say? "You spent an hour learning how to relax! And your homework assignment is to relax for 15 minutes before every study session!" Yeah, right.

Dr. Jacobsen's theory was that by completely relaxing

the muscles of your body, you would also relax your mind. But how does one know when they have completely relaxed their muscles? The electroencephalograph tells us that many people think they are fully relaxed when they aren't. It's the hidden tension that fools them. This is the tension that inhibits concentration when studying, and memory recall when testing. Many students fall into this category.

How many friends do you know who would admit to being uptight prior to a test? Come on! It's not "cool" being uptight. But it is reality unless you know how to relax and win, not deny your tension.

RELAXATION TECHNIQUES THAT WORK

Yoga, meditation, music, prayer, guided imagery—there are many effective techniques that allow you to totally relax your muscles and accelerate the communication with your subconscious mind. My best results have come from using therapeutic hypnosis, as it enables me to send re-programming messages for releasing anxiety and accelerating learning.

In order to teach these techniques in workshops, I have adapted the most powerful programming aspects of therapeutic hypnosis and incorporated them into a user-friendly form of self-hypnosis, which I refer to as "Suggestive Relaxation." Very similar to therapeutic hypnosis in that once your muscles are thoroughly relaxed, suggestions are given to your subconscious mind. The most significant difference—with Suggestive Relaxation, you control the suggestions.

It is as basic as being able to create new mental images in your conscious mind. Once you've created these new images, you simply suggest them as new instructions to your subconscious mind—suggestions like being able to concentrate fully and absorb knowledge when studying, or having total memory recall when testing. Imagine, suggesting to yourself that you are living your most immediate Master Dream!

You are going to learn the five basic techniques that make up Suggestive Relaxation. This will provide you with a working knowledge that can be put to immediate use. But first it is important for you to recognize and understand your relationship with pressure and stress. The following profile will enable you to reflect, be honest with yourself (this isn't an exercise in "cool") and therefore get more benefit from Suggestive Relaxation.

SSP: STUDENT STRESS PROFILE

	Strongly Agree	Mildly Agree	Mildly Disagree	Strongly Disagree
1. I have trouble concentrating when I study.	4	3	2	1
2. I get extremely nervous about tests.	4	3	2	1
3. I often have headaches because of schoolwork.	4	3	2	1
4. I have trouble sleeping before a big test.	4	3	2	1
5. My heart races whenever I'm called on in class.	4	3	2	1
6. I'm very concerned about what my friends think.	4	3	2	1

7. My parents are always putting pressure on me.	4	3	2	1
8. I have trouble communicating with my parents.	4	3	2	1
9. I worry a lot.	4	3	2	1
10. I don't let people know how I really feel.	4	3	2	1

Maximum Score = 40   My Score_____

Score:

40–36   You are in a pressure-cooker. Master the contents of this chapter immediately.

35–29   You're almost in the pressure-cooker. You had best pay attention to your tension levels or you're headed for problems.

28–21   Average. But you can certainly improve how you deal with stress.

20–14   You are doing well. Enjoy the exercises in this chapter and assist your Dream Team Buddy in this area.

13–10   You are amazing! Remember to maintain your commitment to your Master Dream List.

In your Mind Power Notebook list the areas where you have a need for improvement. Review your responses on the Profile and select three specific areas that you need to strengthen. Discuss these areas with your buddy to make certain you are targeting your efforts properly. Now let's take a close look at Suggestive Relaxation. . . .

SUGGESTIVE RELAXATION: FIVE EASY TECHNIQUES

1. Breathing
2. Relaxation
3. Imagery
4. Reprogramming
5. The Control Flame

My method of teaching Suggestive Relaxation is to break the exercise down into its individual component parts, teach exercises that enable mastery of each part, and then bring all the parts together into one suggestive relaxation exercise. Don't worry, it's a lot easier than I just made it appear. But you must master each step, so please don't skip over the individual exercises. Suggestive Relaxation is simple but not easy. Many people breathe incorrectly, are not able to relax their minds and bodies, and don't practice any form of controlled imagery or visualization techniques. Which is why most people are not in control of their lives.

Please bear with me as I emphasize the obvious. You are to master each step, one step at a time, before attempting to complete the Suggestive Relaxation exercise in its entirety. If you are familiar with these various techniques, you will be practicing Suggestive Relaxation in short order. But if you aren't, this will save you considerable frustration, as you would ultimately be forced to begin anew, for failure in mastering Suggestive Relaxation will severely handicap accomplishing your dreams. So relax (ha!), you are about to learn a Mind Power exercise that will keep you free of negative pressure and stress. It's another big step in gaining control of your life. Take your time and have **fun**!

TECHNIQUE NUMBER 1: BREATHING

Without it no mammal could survive, for breath is life. We can go weeks without food, days without water, but only minutes without air. If you are like most people, you've taken breathing for granted, and have developed the habit of breathing incorrectly. You pull in your stomach, and puff out your chest, looking good in terms of posture, but poor in terms of breathing.

Any time you stand with your stomach held in and your chest puffed out, most of your air remains high in your chest. Your lungs are then never fully utilized. Unfortunately, this interferes with your natural physiological relaxation response, which is essential to suggestive relaxation.

Breathing through your stomach, or diaphragmatic breathing, is the way you were designed to breathe, which makes it very easy to learn. All you have to do is fill your lungs completely with air, starting in your stomach (diaphragm). I call it "belly breathing" because your stomach fills with air first, therefore puffing out, before your chest fills and puffs.

Watch a baby breathe—that little belly just continues to rise and fall in perfect rhythm. A sleeping dog, albeit usually a bigger belly, has the same rhythm. It's nature's way. Okay, I know you've got the idea. But what's the big deal about breathing? You've made it this far in life without it seeming to get in your way. Or has it? Let's rethink that statement. If you are under too much pressure and stress, if you worry too much, if you get uptight before taking a test, or simply studying for a test, the odds are that you breathe improperly.

Breathing oxygenates your mind and body. Having the ability to relax, thereby causing more oxygen to travel through your body and to your brain, boosts confidence in the midst of pressure and provides more clarity of mind. It facilitates concentration, knowledge absorption, and memory recall—all the vital components of organized education.

As Taisen Deshimaru writes in *The Zen Way to Martial Arts* (E. P. Dutton, 1982), ''Air contains the energy of life and the life from the universe which we receive through our lungs and every cell in our bodies, so it is important to know how to breathe.''

BREATHING PRACTICE SESSION

Step 1:

- Lie on the floor in a quiet place where you will not be disturbed for 10 minutes.
- Place your hands on your stomach, directly below your rib cage.
- Take a deep breath.
- Notice how your hands move, if at all. If they move up and down with each breath, you are belly breathing—filling your stomach with air first.

Step 2:

- Concentrate on emptying your lungs completely as you breathe.
- Monitor your breathing pattern as you inhale, stomach expanding, upper stomach and chest expanding, and finally filling the upper portion of your lungs.

Step 3:

- Concentrate on your exhalations.
- Empty your lungs completely.

- Do you exhale through your mouth or through your nose?
- Determine whether you are exhaling through your mouth or nose.

Step 4:

- Take a full breath, inhaling through your nose.
- Exhale completely through your mouth.
- Repeat this pattern until it feels comfortable.

Step 5:

- Practice Step 4 until you can breathe naturally in this pattern, inhaling fully through your nose, and exhaling completely through your mouth.

Welcome to the world of belly breathing! It will help you score higher on any test. I promise!

TECHNIQUE NUMBER 2: RELAXATION

It was during the original Woodstock era when the first wave of relaxation, in the form of transcendental meditation, crashed onto the American shores. Relaxation thus grabbed people's attention, gaining a place of importance in the minds of many. Known as TM, the Western world began to hear testimonials from famous athletes, Hollywood stars, and a vast array of public figures attesting to the value relaxation brought to their lives. They seemed to validate the belief that the mind controls the body, and by relaxing the mind and body, one could improve almost every aspect of life.

A few years following the TM craze, a Harvard physician, Herbert Benson, published his research on relaxation in what was to become the best-selling *Relaxation Response* (Morrow, 1975). Dr. Benson legitimized the claims of TM and its followers, but offered a more practical form of teaching relaxation in his book, at a much more affordable price—the cost of his book. Yet relaxation, and all its benefits, remains one of those abstract concepts whose value is recognized by many but practiced by few. Now is the time to practice.

RELAXATION PRACTICE SESSION

Step 1:

- Get a relaxing piece of music playing in the background.
- Find a quiet spot where you will not be interrupted for 15 minutes.
- Sit in a straight-backed chair, feet flat on the floor, hands lying loosely in your lap. (This gives you an upright spinal alignment, essential to yoga and meditation.)

Step 2:

- Take four to five belly breaths.
- Concentrate on each inhalation, each exhalation, and your relaxation response.

Step 3:

- Clench your jaw firmly, closing it as tightly as you can.
- While maintaining this clenched position, note the muscles at work.
- Let yourself become aware of the sensations in your neck and face.
- Notice the tension created: tightness in your lower back, stomach, butt, legs, and breathing.
- Release your jaw, let it sag and go loose.

- Wiggle your jaw, let it sag and go loose again.
- Relax your jaw.

Step 4:

- Clench your jaw again and repeat the entire process.
- Be aware of all the sensations associated with this extreme tension and subsequent relaxation.
- Repeat Step 3, the clenching exercise, with any muscle group: fist, thigh, etc.
- Your objective is to be able to recognize tension vs. relaxation.

Step 5:

- Take two belly breaths.
- Close your eyes.
- Picture your feet in your mind, as you concentrate on your breathing. Feel them relax.
- Next, take your mind into your legs, picturing and feeling your calves, knees, and thighs relaxing.
- Picture your stomach, as it is often a center of tension and stress. Simply feel your muscle loosening.
- Take your mind into your back, all they way down your spine, letting loose each step of the way. (This is another storage area for tension and stress.)
- Picture your neck, yet another magnet of tension, and let it relax.

Step 6:

- Practice Step 5 until you feel comfortable with the progressive relaxation.
- Take your time. You can not rush relaxation,

rather simply get accustomed to the process when
exercised in its entirety.
* Enjoy!

There is no one way to relax. Soothing music is very
helpful for most people, but if you don't like relaxing to
music, skip the music. Think of this practice session as
simply a guide. Because that's exactly what it is.

TECHNIQUE NUMBER 3: IMAGERY

Here is where the fun really begins. Using your imagination, that ability to daydream creatively. I've already
involved your imagination with the crystal ball exercise
in Chapter 1. Remember looking into that crystal ball,
beginning with the end in mind, regarding those three areas you selected? That exercised your imagination. You
are going to spend a lot of time imagining your dreams.
This will take some work, as it is not an idle daydream,
rather a structured process. But it's still a blast!

Much like relaxation, there is no right way of imaging.
Some people are more visual than others. It's easy for
some to picture themselves at the beach, while others can
only think of being at the beach. Other people are more
auditory and might bring various sounds, such as the
ocean, into the imagery. Still others are more kinesthetic
and tend to "feel" things as a sensory experience, such
as running on the beach, the movement of the waves, or
the feel of the sand.

Although you probably find one of these easier than the
others, you have the ability to imagine them all. Try it.
Imagine lying on the sand at the beach, feel the heat from
both the sand and the sun. Now hear the sound of the
ocean, the cry of seagulls, the sound of the wind,

TECHNIQUE NUMBER 4: REPROGRAMMING

Finally! You've relaxed your mind and body sufficiently, exercised your imagination with complete sensory details, and now you're ready to program what you want in your subconscious. Here is where you're going to create specific mental images that correspond directly to your Master Dream List, your immediate goals—the subject of the next chapter.

You might feel the tendency to skip over this section and move right into synergistic goal-setting. Don't! Relaxation and imagery are skills that you need to practice with, if only briefly. The more sensory detail, the more you can guarantee your goals becoming reality. If you can see, feel, touch, taste, and hear them, you can take them to the bank!

You are now going to want to feel comfortable with your ability to create the necessary mental images, in sensory detail, of what you want. Naturally, this means you will need to be specific in your goals, but before I have you zeroing in on time-specific, measurable goals, I'd like you to practice imagining big—visualizing your wildest expectations, you know, like Arnold did. As with any new skill, this requires a little practice.

Yes, you can do it!

Although each component part of Suggestive Relaxation is simple, you might experience some frustration along the way. You're exercising something that is intangible—your mind. Because of this, there's no definitive measuring point to chart your progress. Just keep an eye on the most immediate dreams linked to your fixed daily activities—such as your grades beginning to improve, your work-outs intensifying, etc. Don't be concerned if you can't see all of your dream images, just keep practicing—they will come. Also, there's no such thing as perfection. By simply relaxing and thinking about what you want, you're sending programming signals to your subconscious, even if you can't visualize them. But I'm certain you can!

BUDDY EXERCISE: Use your Mind Power Notebook to write and picture your feelings and then go over this with your Dream Team, if you have one.

PICTURE YOURSELF A WINNER

1. See yourself as a confident, capable person doing a specific activity associated with your most immediate dream, one that you really want to do well. Picture yourself going through the motions of performing that activity and enjoying it immensely (studying, shooting baskets, public speaking, etc.).
   Write your picture and feelings:_____
   _____
   _____

2. Picture yourself completely relaxed, listening to music by yourself.
   Write your picture and feelings:_____
   _____
   _____

3. Picture yourself accomplishing your most immediate dream.
   Write your picture and feelings:_____
   _____
   _____

4. Imagine yourself standing in front of your class with high self-esteem, full of confidence.
   Write your picture and feelings:_____
   _____
   _____

5. Picture yourself shaking hands with your role model, as equals.
   Write your picture and feelings:_____
   _____
   _____

REPROGRAMMING PRACTICE SESSION:

- Sit in your straight-backed chair position.
- Take two belly breaths.
- Relax your entire body.
- Create your private peaceful image scene.
- Picture yourself as a high self-esteem achiever.
- Picture yourself as that high self-esteem achiever going through your upcoming day. See yourself interacting with loving care to your family and friends. See yourself performing the activities of a high self-esteem achiever.
- Imagine yourself studying with complete concentration and absorbing knowledge, testing with total confidence, and having total memory recall; imagine yourself getting the grades you want, getting the job of your dreams.

(**Note:** These are the same techniques Olympic athletes use to "see themselves through" their best performances. They form a mental image of themselves doing their best; then they go through the motions of doing what they've just daydreamed. It works!)

TECHNIQUE NUMBER 5: THE CONTROL FLAME

It's important to turn tension into concentration that enables you to absorb knowledge when studying. One of the reasons so many students don't achieve their dreams is that they get overwhelmed with the tension and stress of learning; homework, studying, and taking tests. Can you relate? You try to fight these strong feelings with logic, emotions with reason. You may tell yourself to relax while taking a test, but your nervous system doesn't buy it.

The more you try to deny the tension, the more debilitating it becomes, until finally it consumes you. This has been the primary cause of test-choking or school "burnout." Here's a wonderful tool that can reverse all this tension.

YOUR MENTAL SIGNAL

Imagine this scenario: You're about ready to sit down and study for a big test. Normally, you would be feeling a bit uptight, worried about the test, and forcing yourself to "get it over with." Instead of fighting these feelings of nervous tension/anxiety/worry with logic, you imagine the flame of a candle; take one full belly breath; visualize releasing those negative feelings as you exhale; and affirm to yourself, "I'm relaxed, have total concentration, and absorb knowledge."

You cannot have two thoughts in your mind at the same time. It's impossible! Many students think they have dozens of thoughts racing through their minds all at once— lessons, homework assignments, boyfriends, girlfriends, tests, deadlines—when really their conscious minds are simply working extremely fast, much too fast.

You have already learned about affirmations and self-talk in Chapter 2. In Chapter 3 you learned how to make your most powerful self-help tape. By this time I would expect that you have been listening to, and experiencing the benefits of, this powerful tool. For the purpose of your control flame, "I am relaxed with total concentration and absorb knowledge'' is a perfect programming statement prior to every studying session.

This is how it works:

You recognize negative tension and . . .

- immediately visualize the flame of a candle
- concentrate as you exhale, seeing yourself blowing out the flame, and at the same time, blowing out your negative tension
- then say to yourself, ''I'm relaxed with total concentration and absorb knowledge.''

Here is another good Dream Team exercise. Both you and your buddy can write down a situation where your nerves interfered with your learning performance. Be as specific as possible. Let your buddy read this stressful re-creation and you simply use your control flame. Practice with it—it's fun and extremely powerful.

Consider the control flame your private mental signal. It can be the most versatile Mind Power technique you will ever encounter. I've used it with compulsive eaters, professional athletes, dancers, salespeople, pilots, you name it. You can effectively deal with any negative thought or emotion by using your control flame coupled with a full belly breath. Used properly, it can flip your Mind Power switch from destructive to constructive in a matter of seconds.

In the next chapter, I'm going to show you how to apply the power of Suggestive Relaxation to your daily goal-getting program. Synergistic goal-getting is the ultimate Mind Power tool for turning your wildest expectations, goals, into a mental compulsion. And what a compulsion!

WRAP-UP

- Relaxation improves subconscious programming.
- Belly breathing is critical to your natural relaxation response.
- Many people are not aware of their level of tension.
- Studying and testing creates a lot of tension.
- Excess tension interferes with concentration and hinders memory recall.
- Suggestive Relaxation is a nonthreatening method of relaxing the conscious mind and body in preparation for programming.
- Your control flame will help you turn tension into relaxed concentration to absorb knowledge and have natural memory recall.
- Practice all five techniques of Suggestive Relaxation.

Chapter 9

Synergistic Goal-Getting

"The most important thing about goals is having one."

—Geoffery F. Albert

Now that you've discovered how good it feels to relax completely and tune into your subconscious mind, let's move ahead to the next step: creating a powerful goal-getting exercise by harmonizing the powers of your conscious and subconscious mind. You will need to understand their different roles.

GOAL-GETTING

CONSCIOUS ROLE:

This is where your Master Dream List is refined into measurable, time-specific targets. These become your goals. Once you have consciously determined your goals, you are ready to engage in a daily goal-getting exercise. Your conscious role is to write out your entiregoal statement; longrange (3 to 5 years), intermediate (immediate to 1 year), and fixed daily activities.

This simple exercise in writing sends a strong sensory message to your brain—like when you write down your homework assignments but don't even need to check your written reminder because you remember it clearly. You wouldn't have been as likely to remember if you had not written down the assignment.

SUBCONSCIOUS ROLE:

At this stage of your Mind Power development you should have a fairly good idea of the subconscious role. Here is where you take your consciously written goal statements and spend 10 to 15 minutes using Suggestive Relaxation to visualize the exact goals you have written down in as much detail as possible. You will be amazed at the increase of sensory detail in your visual images because of taking the time to consciously write your goal statements.

By writing and then visualizing what you have written, you will be reprogramming your subconscious mind to accept a new and more successful vision of yourself, a vision that you have carefully sculptured. Like any good sculptor, you will be refining your success image as you continue working with it. But it is through this harmony of Mind Power that you will ultimately bring this vision to reality. You will accelerate changes in both attitude and behavior by changing the way you see yourself. You will act with more confidence, you will consistently improve your performance, and your success image will continue to grow stronger. This is truly exciting!

Very few people, students or adults, practice any type of a regular goal-getting exercise. And if they do, it's usually nothing more than looking over an annual goal statement every so often. This is absurd! Would you have ever learned to read in elementary school if you merely glanced at your books once in a while? Do you think your Master Dream List will become a reality if you only glance at it on occasion? Of course not!

Think of it like this, you are about to burn your wildest expectations—your goals—deep into your being, into your psychic consciousness. They will become second nature to you just like your ability to read the words on this page. During the 20 minutes in which you will be living your goals, you will be actively exercising your mind, conscious and subconscious. This is the ultimate in constructive Mind Power. This is why I know that your dreams, those wild expectations, will become your mental compulsion. And what a compulsion!

In other words, Suggestive Relaxation does more than keep you free of negative tension. It opens the door to your subconscious. Your subconscious mind is prepared to receive whatever signals you want to send. This is why the role your conscious mind plays is so very important: it determines the signals you send. These signals take the form of specific goal statements—phrases that help stimulate the pleasant mental images associated with achieving your goals. You will be seeing yourself living up to your wildest expectations, those goals you've written.

VISUALIZE YOUR WILDEST EXPECTATIONS—YOUR DREAMS

"To do much clear thinking one must arrange for regular periods of solitude in order to indulge the imagination without distraction."
—Thomas Alva Edison

Given the opportunity, everyone would love to live their dreams. Unfortunately, realizing those wildest of expectations remains only a pipe dream for most people. Why? Because they have never really learned to believe they can achieve such lofty goals. They can not see themselves, in their own image, succeeding because they haven't taken the time to strategically exercise the theater of their mind. They have not accepted the starring role in their mental theater by experiencing their dreams in minute detail through visualization. In previous chapters, you were involved with a bit of visual imagery during those crystal ball exercises. Now it's time to make certain those successful images come more naturally and more consistently.

Controlling the theater in your mind, your imagination, takes a bit of practice. But actually it's both simple in concept and easy in application. Like anything you become good at, it requires disciplined practice. Master these exercises, perform the final version daily, and nothing will hold you back. You will get whatever you want out of life.

Okay. Take each of the following statements separately, read the statement, take two belly breaths, close your eyes and then visualize the statement you have just read. Spend a couple of minutes with each statement.

1. Picture yourself doing something really great in your immediate future. See yourself full of confidence and positive energy, feeling good about yourself in every way, going through the motions in great detail of doing this task very well. Whether it's scoring the touchdown, climbing a mountain, giving a speech to your class, giving a recital, or taking a test, create this image in your mind.
2. Imagine yourself standing in front of a mirror admiring your success image.
3. Visualize yourself being congratulated by your friends, teachers, coaches, and family for your great achievement.

You can discuss this exercise with your buddy. Are the images coming naturally? Are you able to create sensory detail (sound, touch, smell)? Do you sense that you are forcing these images in your mind?

At this stage in your Mind Power development various images will flow more freely into your mind. Your ability to concentrate on the images you desire, while filtering out the rest, will come with practice. If either you or your buddy are experiencing any problems with these images, chill out, you're probably trying too hard. An important point to keep in mind regarding the theater in your mind—there is no perfection in visualization. If you continue to struggle, as many adults do, revisit all five techniques of Suggestive Relaxation outlined in the previous chapter.

Whatever your wildest expectations, whatever immediate dreams you might have linked to these wild expectations, whatever fixed daily activities you've got linked to these dreams, in your visualizations you will see yourself successfully accomplishing all of this, every day. This is powerful stuff! The clearer your mental pictures, the more these pictures will work for you. This is how Mind Power works. Detailed visual images send a stronger signal to your subconscious mind than vague images.

Couple this with your 7-7-7 Tape and not only are you reprogramming your mind, you are changing the way you see yourself. You are creating the exact self-image you have always wanted.

Once you are able to operate in the theater in your mind and can visualize yourself living your dreams on demand, you are prepared for synergistic goal-getting. Notice I never talk about setting goals, it's all about getting goals! You are about to directly involve both your conscious and subconscious mind as allies in your dream quest.

SYNERGISTIC GOAL-GETTING

Whenever you hear the word synergy think of $2 + 2 = 5$. Basically, it describes a situation where the whole is greater than the sum of all individual parts. I have taken a liking to using this word to explain the force created from getting the conscious and subconscious mind to work together in getting goals. That's why I refer to it as sort of a "$2 + 2 = 5$" kind of thing.

What you are about to learn will enable you to engage all of this awesome mental power you've been reading about to become that person in your dreams—to live up to your wildest expectations. Synergistic goal-getting is a two-step exercise that starts with your conscious mind establishing specific written goals. You have already been heavily involved with your conscious mind in creating your Master Dream List and immediate dream accomplishments. Once you have consciously committed all of this to writing, the next step is to be able to subconsciously create some form of a pictorial representation of these future accomplishments.

There are tricks to help you with a real image of your dreams, a pictorial representation. What I have found to be the simplest and most effective is an actual picture that represents your accomplishment. For instance, if you want to become a doctor you might get a photograph of a hospital and place your picture with the words Dr._____ and the date you plan on being a licensed physician. Mary Lou Retton, the 1984 United States Olympic gold medalist in gymnastics, mentally pictured herself conducting her perfect ''10'' winning routine over and over long before her actual performance, and her sparkling personality and smile entered the homes of sports fans throughout the world. Most likely she had some sort of picture of herself with an Olympic gold medal draped around her neck over her bed as part of her mental training routine. Once you get past thinking this exercise is corny, you'll realize it is extremely powerful in helping you create detailed visual images of your future accomplishments.

With all these preliminaries taken care of, you are ready for Suggestive Relaxation—the subconscious part. Let's get started.

WRITING YOUR GOALS

Go back to your Mind Power Notebook and review your Master Dream List. Are you comfortable with your most immediate dream accomplishments? If not, now is the time to make any necessary changes. Ditto to the fixed daily activities linked to these accomplishments. Review them and make certain everything is appropriate.

Now you are ready to transform your dreams from the abstract, your wish list, into time-specific and measurable targets. This gives dreams virtual reality and transforms them into goals that have a beginning and an end. The mechanics for synergistic goal-getting will be outlined later in the chapter, as I've always found it useful to first provide a conceptual overview of the entire process.

The idea is to begin long-range and work toward the immediate. So first you would want to select a long-range goal from your Master Dream List. For most students this is fairly sequential, as your second step in synergistic goal-getting is to select an accomplishment you would like a year from now. This would likely be one of your more immediate dream accomplishments—it might be acceptance into the college of your choice, becoming the starting point guard, getting into graduate school, and so on. I refer to these one-year targets as *intermediate goals*. The long-range targets might vary from graduating college, to getting a job, to having a family. What you are doing with this exercise is forcing yourself to look into the future with a time-frame in mind. Hey, three to five years isn't that far off. You are strengthening your accountability.

Everything is linked. Your intermediate goal is a stepping-stone to your long-range goals, and your fixed daily activities are the steps you will take to achieving your intermediate goals.

CREATING BALANCED GOALS

"A healthy poor man is half a rich one."
—Chinese proverb

Establishing goal-getting targets is a bit different than creating your Master Dream List. First of all, you are dealing with those top-priority, most immediate dreams—admission to the college of your choice, being the starting point guard, graduation from college, or graduate school, starting a career, etc. Secondly, you don't need to involve all four areas of your Master Dream List (professional, personal, family, spiritual). Select two. This will provide more than enough balance to get you started in getting your dreams. Whether it's personal and professional, professional and family, or professional and spiritual . . . you need balance. My experience has been that most students select professional and personal goals. It's your call.

You will find it helpful to write your goals in two ways. Take one page of your Mind Power Notebook and list the actual results you want to achieve. On the following page, list the sensory and emotional components of those results—how it looks, feels, sounds, smells, and tastes to reach your goals. You know, the sweet taste of victory. In this manner, you will be dealing with both your conscious and subconscious mind.

I can remember Kurt, a high school junior who was a terrific tennis player but always seemed to choke during tournaments. In addition to wanting a tennis scholarship to college, Kurt had always wanted to be a lawyer. When it came to writing his goals, he was fine with the actual results, but found difficulty creating sensory images that involved being a lawyer. It was easy for him to conjure up the emotions associated with winning the upcoming tennis tournament. He could see himself being interviewed by the local newspaper, feel the hugs of congratulations from his coach and teammates, and imagine the victory dinner his mother would prepare for the entire family. But sensory images of being a lawyer . . . ? Not easy.

It wasn't until Kurt actually won this tournament that he was able to recognize the power of sensory images. His victory was a déjà vu experience—he had already been there in great sensory detail in his mind. From this basis of understanding he was able to give his mind creative license in becoming a lawyer. Using the movie *The*

Firm as his guide, he sensed the plush office, smelled the leather chairs, and saw himself driving his new BMW while wearing an expensive Italian suit.

As he explained to me, "Winning the tournament opened my mind and relieved a lot of pressure. I could relate to the power of detailed sensory imagery as it really helped me overcome choking. I had choked so often in the past, but somehow I knew was going to win—it was weird. So now I've started having fun with the images of being a lawyer."

Like Kurt, you might find it easier to create sensory images with one of your goal-getting targets. That's okay. Regardless, your conscious mind still receives the benefits from the written message and your subconscious mind is still being programmed to propel you forward. Rich visual images will come in time. So make certain to relax and have fun. Remember, you're dealing with your wildest expectations, but only in the short term. Arnold Schwarzenegger saw himself in great sensory detail as both Mr. Universe and a Hollywood movie star.

Let's take a look at Kurt's original goal statements. Naturally yours will be different, but reading through his statements will help you get started. First, I will take you through his specific goal statements, then I'll share the sensory components to his goals.

WRITING GOAL-GETTING STATEMENTS

Long-range (5 years): I am enrolled at Wake Forest Law School

Intermediate (1 year): I have a full tennis scholarship at the UNC—Chapel Hill

Immediate (2 months): I win the regional tennis tournament; (4 months): I score 1150 on my SATs.

Fixed Daily Activities:

- I drill hard for 1 hour on the tennis courts before school (6:30–7:30 A.M.)
- I spend 2 quality hours studying in the library.
- I work hard for the entire 2-hour tennis practice.
- I lift weights for 20 minutes of circuit training.
- I ride the exercise bike for 30 minutes to keep my legs strong.
- I spend 2 to 3 quality hours doing my homework after dinner.

Using Kurt's goal-getting exercise as a model, I want you to note how he then uses his imagination to create the sensory components of each goal in the following exercise. The idea is to write the feelings you expect to experience as you accomplish your goal. Kurt is recording exactly what he imagines it would be like to be there, living his accomplishments. This is a one-time exercise which will assist you in creating the sensory-rich details in his daily Suggestive Relaxation exercise.

KURT'S WRITTEN SENSORY GOAL EXERCISE

Kurt's long-range target was to be a law student at Wake Forest University. His intermediate goal was to win a tennis tournament, for which it was easier for him to create sensory images. Here is how he was finally able to translate his goal of becoming a law student into sensory messages that would strengthen the communication to his subconscious mind.

Sight: I pictured myself walking to class with fellow law students, arms full of law books, on a beautiful North Carolina spring day.

Sound:	I listened, and participated in, a stimulating discussion on criminal law.
Touch:	I could feel the knowledge contained by the weight of my law books.
Smell:	I relished breathing the fresh spring air as I walked.
Emotions:	I felt pride in being a law student and the thought of soon becoming a lawyer.

A FIXED DAILY ACTIVITY

"There are no gains without pains."
—Benjamin Franklin

To ensure the magic of synergistic goal-getting is working for you, you must reinforce your daily commitment to get your goals. I have a simple and proven method that will enable you to do just that. I refer to it as the 20-Minute Solution. You don't have to make this exercise a daily activity to enjoy the benefits, a couple times a week will do the trick, but if you want to accelerate the entire process, make this a fixed daily activity—you will be amazed at the results!

You'll need a notebook with space to rewrite your goals. Your Mind Power Notebook coupled with one of your daily school notebooks can serve this purpose. Simply earmark a page approximately halfway through your Mind Power Notebook and label it "Goal-Getting." Every day you are going to rewrite your long-range and intermediate goals, in the same style Kurt wrote his above. Next you'll switch to your daily school notebook, flip to your upcoming day, and write your fixed daily activities—just as Kurt has written his.

Notice that Kurt's written statements are worded as affirmations. He has even written exactly how he wants to study after dinner. In order to maximize the value of this exercise you must write every statement as an affirmation, present tense positive, just like when you made your affirmation tape. Set aside five to seven minutes to write your goals as I have described. This is only half of the synergistic goal-getting exercise; the remainder (13 to 15 minutes) involves Suggestive Relaxation.

REWRITING GOALS

Every time you write goal statements, begin with the end in mind. In other words, write your long-range state-ment first and work backwards to your fixed daily activities. This should take between five and seven minutes.

Many people wonder why they have to rewrite the same goal statements every day. The answer is simple: If you want your goals to become a mental compulsion, if you want them etched into your heart and soul, if you want to make certain you get them—it's a basic requirement. Every day? Well, at least five days a week—nobody's perfect.

Make certain to keep your long-range goals within the three- to five-year time table. Your intermediate goals can be anything from a couple of months, to some time closer to your long-range goals, as they must be accomplished before your long-range goals. Your fixed daily activities serve as your action plan for each day. Keep these state-ments short and make certain they are always written as affirmation statements. Kurt, for example, is already a law student in his subconscious mind.

There are many other bonuses that come with the 20-Minute Solution. It serves as a time-management tool, as you manage yourself through each day, making certain you have a productive day. You are also in touch with your Master Dream List, to which this entire goal-getting exercise is merely a subset. Probably the most important bonus is the release of stress. You will be purging your system of negative stress every day. In effect, as you transform your goals into a mental compulsion, you are also flushing your mind and body of toxicity and realigning your internal resources. This is the essence of Mind Power.

Yes, every day you will write the same goals, in the same sequence, in your Mind Power Notebook. You will then write your fixed daily activities for the day in your daily planner. Every day these positive images will be reinforced in your subconscious mind. But there's more. The next step will allow you to live these dreams in advance.

RELAX AND IMAGINE YOUR DAY

Your goal-getting exercise is not complete until you add Suggestive Relaxation. And the good news is you already know how to do it. Simply follow the steps of Technique Number 4: Reprogramming, in Chapter 7. Just take about 15 minutes to relax and visualize what you've just written. Everything is linked. Now let's put it all together.

SYNERGISTIC GOAL-GETTING

1. **Write your goal statements:**

   - *Long-range* (3 to 5 years into the future, one step beyond your most immediate dream accomplishment—maximum four sentences)
   - *Intermediate* (1 year ahead, likely to be your most immediate dream accomplishment—maximum four sentences)

- *Immediate* (upcoming test, etc.)
- *Fixed daily activities* (your daily routine that will lead you to your intermediate goal)

2. **Suggestive Relaxation:**

- Sit in your straight-backed chair.
- Take two belly breaths and close your eyes.
- Relax your entire body.
- Create your private peaceful image.
- Picture yourself living your long-range goal, exactly as you've written it, with as much sensory detail as possible. See yourself there.
- Visualize yourself living your intermediate goal with as much sensory detail as possible.
- See yourself going through your entire day, doing each of your fixed daily activities, in sensory detail, just as you'd like to do them.

This entire goal-getting exercise should take no longer than 20 minutes. But take your time; it's important that you complete it in an unhurried manner. Once you've finished the exercise, get on with your day as usual.

Think of this as not only the ultimate mental exercise, but the ultimate exercise. A strong mind is far superior than a strong body. The mind controls the body. It can make it sick or healthy, bring about confidence or bring on depression. The mind is both your King and Queen. It is your royalty. Which is why you will amaze yourself within only a couple of weeks of practicing this exercise. You will begin to see results. One step at a time and you will find yourself getting your goals.

It is not unusual for people to discover they need to revise their intermediate goals because they have reached them early. Jack has been accepted to college. Sally's grades have improved to where she wanted them. Billy won the tournament, made the team, and so on. This is cool. I love watching Mind Power at work, but these students must accept the new challenge of creating new goals that are still linked to their long-range goals and to their original Master Dream List.

Is this magic? Are you guaranteed to get every goal? No. But I can guarantee that you will be in control of your life and be far better off for being actively involved in this goal-getting exercise. Some people do not get all of their goals. Well, that's life. But as long as they were actively striving to achieve, only good will result. I can remember not getting accepted into the law school of my choice. Although it was my mother's goal more than mine, I went into private counseling and got a master's degree at night school. The net result was very positive. Heck, I didn't have to become a lawyer! The secret is working towards goals that are linked to your Master Dream List.

Keep practicing your daily Suggestive Relaxation as part of your daily goal-getting exercise. This way you're killing those two proverbial birds with one stone: you're learning how to relax and win while you're turning your dreams into a mental compulsion.

To help you put this goal-getting exercise in perspective, it's like daily sit-ups for the mind. People who do sit-ups every day have strong stomachs. People who do their goal-getting exercise every day have strong minds. Neither takes much time, yet both require ongoing application. Think of it as taking positive steps, daily, to take total control of your life. Sure, there will be challenges along the way. Nothing in life is free. Overcoming obstacles is the price you must pay.

As you stay with your goal-getting exercise, good things will happen over time. You will gain confidence in both the technique and your ability to use it properly. You will also find that it can rather quickly elevate your self-confidence and change your entire attitude toward yourself, your family, teachers, and school.

Since your goal-getting exercise is the fixed daily activity that drives the other fixed daily activities, make certain your Dream Team Buddy agrees to be held accountable, and holds you accountable, for doing this fixed daily activity. It's hard to imagine doing your goal-getting exercise and having a slack day. Why? Because it won't happen.

Here are some tips that will help you turn this goal getting exercise into a habit:

1. Don't try to reason it all out. The important thing is not the detail surrounding how it works, but that it does work, and will work for you.
2. Don't evaluate yourself. Let both your body relaxation and visualization occur naturally. Guide, don't force. Your mind will wander; gently guide it back to your goal images.
3. Forget about the time. The time guidelines I've provided are just that, guidelines. Some people can do the entire exercise in 10 minutes, for others it might take 30 minutes. Develop your own pace based on your ability to relax your body and make the exercise enjoyable.
4. There are no shortcuts! So don't even look. This exercise has been scientifically developed and carefully tested with thousands of people.
5. Follow the instructions completely. There is a reason behind everything, even the straight-backed chair. Relaxing in a straight-backed chair forces you to exercise your mind, whereas

a comfortable chair might relax you, but rather than exercise your mind, you might find yourself falling asleep without gaining the benefits you want.

6. Discuss this goal-getting exercise with your Dream Team Buddy and other friends who might want to get more out of life—even your parents. You are not hiding anything. Although goal-getting is personal and private, it can become more powerful when you get excited and begin spreading the word. . . .

7. Don't look for a quick fix. Results will come quickly enough simply by doing. You didn't develop into your current state overnight and you won't become a high self-esteem achiever in 24 hours. It takes about three weeks to break an old pattern, and about six weeks to establish a new one. Put your time in and you will be rewarded.

8. Don't struggle with your current self-image. Relax and trust this Mind Power exercise, it is the ultimate and it will work for you!

9. Build Suggestive Relaxation into your daily routine. Make it part of your everyday life: belly breathing, control flame, and muscle relaxation.

10. Persist! Real progress comes with application over time. Stay with it and you will control your life.

Congratulations! You've distanced yourself from 99 percent of the human population. You now have the ability to control the awesome power of the mind in order to live your wildest expectations. Simple, isn't it? All it involves is doing activities you've been doing in some form or other throughout your life, but doing them in a structured way. Everyone dreams, everyone can relax, everyone has planned activities for an upcoming day. So listen clearly, all you "cool dudes"—work this process and it will work for you!

Mind Power for students is actually Mind Power for life. You will be using these skills in every aspect of your life, throughout your journey through your Master Dream List. Sure, the specifics of your goal-getting exercise might change, but the results will be consistent. You will have made a habit of setting and getting your goals. You will be living your wildest expectations.

WRAP-UP

- You involve your conscious mind when you write your goals.
- Every written message sends a signal to your brain.
- Your subconscious mind is actively engaged through suggestive relaxation and visualizing the goals you've written.
- A synergy is where the whole is greater than the sum of all individual parts.
- Begin long-range, then intermediate, immediate, and finally your fixed daily activities, both when writing and visualizing your goals.
- Writing a one-time sensory description of your goals will assist in visualizing your goals.
- Goals always become more real when you experience the feelings that accompany their accomplishment.
- Always word your goal statements and fixed daily activities as affirmation statements.

- Goal-getting is the ultimate **fixed daily activity**!
- Hold your Dream Team Buddy, and yourself, accountable for investing 20 minutes a day for this goal-getting exercise.

Chapter 10

Gotta Believe

"Whether you think you can or think you can't—
you are right."

—Henry Ford

To fully appreciate the powers of mind, you have got to believe. And for the most part, you've gotta believe without proof. I mean, let's get real. There are no guarantees in life. The Christopher Columbus story is well known to many. He had a goal to reach "The Indies"—Eastern Asia—by sailing west. It took him about 10 years to get the financial support to act on his goal and he failed because a huge continent was blocking his way. He discovered America by accident.

Yet we honor him still. And rightfully so. He acted on his dream with both persistence and guts, sailing into uncharted waters, oceans of the unknown, believing without any real proof that he would reach his destination. Christopher Columbus had faith. It was through this faith he was able to persist, to persuade others to journey with him, and yet he still never reached his goal. Was he a failure? Of course not! He was a hero in his own time. Amidst many other positive qualities, Columbus was armed with an unyielding faith—he had no guarantees of success.

It is a shame that more adults are not able to fully capitalize on this God-given intangible with limitless potential—the mind. This is amazing when you consider that the mind and its power have been studied throughout all of recorded history. It's not a new discovery; it's yesterday's news. You only fail when you fail to believe. That's guaranteed!

To fully grasp the law of the mind, and persistently apply it to your life, is to gain mastery of a power that defies imagination—precisely the reason you've gotta believe. Every accomplishment made by man has come through mental effort. Breakthroughs in science, technology, medicine, fine arts, athletics have all been the direct result of Mind Power that has been harnessed and applied constructively over time.

Interestingly, an ancient myth cites the greatest sin of mankind as one of omission: neglecting the powers of mind. Alas, not enough people are aware of this sin and therefore are naïve when it comes to using this powerful tool. Notice the sin is not of failure to get every goal; the sin is in not playing the game—not trying.

A GREAT LEAP IN FAITH

"The fact that I can plant a seed and it becomes a flower, share a bit of knowledge and it becomes another's, smile at someone and receive a smile in return, are to me continual spiritual exercises."

—Leo Buscaglia

To capitalize on this God-given power you must have faith. True faith. The ability to believe without proof. This, my friends, is nondenominational faith. There is a lot more to religion than going to church or synagogue or temple or mosque every week. Columbus, a devout, almost fanatical Christian, believed that God had given him talents and prayed for strength, but he couldn't attend church during his voyages.

Your ability to obtain maximum benefit from the powers of mind will be in direct correlation to your faith. You have to do more than dream; you must be capable of believing without proof—believing in yourself, your God-given talents, and your future. In essence, you must accept the fact that there is a force, a greater power, that it's available to everyone who asks.

Understand me clearly on this point. In no way am I selling religion. There are enough people in that game. I am selling the timeless, nondenominational, power of faith. This is essential for you and your Dream Team Buddy. Whether you attend services regularly with your family, worship on a personal level, or are taking a break from organized religion until you begin to raise a family is irrelevant to living your wildest expectations. The true measure of faith is your ability to believe coupled with your willingness to make full use of those talents provided for you at birth. There is no room for skeptics on this issue. Faith allows you to fail while working to get your goals. Nobody succeeds without failure.

THE POWER OF FAITH

I know what some of you are probably thinking. "Come on. Is faith really necessary? Does the ability to believe really have a direct relationship with getting goals?" Allow me to answer these questions by sharing a case from my files. Jerri had been a mother and housewife for the previous 15 years. She raised three children, her youngest was a sophomore in high school, and she was now ready to get a job. She quickly received a rude wake-up call— nobody wanted to hire a housewife with a high school education and no experience.

Undeterred, Jerri decided to follow in the footsteps of a cousin and sell real estate. Everybody encouraged her as she was energetic, outgoing, and knew a lot of people. But there was one obstacle, the real estate licensing exam.

Jerri visited my office after she had failed this exam twice. For all her determination to get a job, it took only a few minutes of listening to her to recognize the heart of her problem.

She had no faith. Oh, she went to church regularly, I'm referring to her faith in her ability to pass exams. "I never liked taking tests. I think it was probably the major reason I avoided college and became a homemaker," she confessed. "But now I've got to pass this real estate exam, and I'm not sure I can."

With that mind-set, what were the odds Jerri would get her real estate license? Slim to none. She was locked in that negative programming cycle with regard to tests. Beneath a positive exterior lurked that bad habit number 1. Yet she still had faith in her ability to sell. The hurdle was expanding this faith to the exam and pushing her into the positive programming cycle. And guess what? It was easy. Jerri visited my office only once and passed the exam, and has gone on to become one of the most successful real estate agents in her city. What changed was her ability to believe, without proof, that she could pass the exam.

How was she able to take this leap of faith? By changing her programming cycle from negative to positive and focusing on doing specific fixed daily activities that were linked to an immediate target (the real estate licensing exam), which was linked to an intermediate goal (becoming a professional real estate agent), which was linked to her long-range goal (earn $100,000 per year selling real estate). Her fixed daily activities involved listening to her affirmation tape, spending 20 minutes in the morning doing her goal-getting exercise, using the control flame, and spending 45 minutes per day studying.

In less than one week of doing these Mind Power activities Jerri had begun to change her programming cycle. She could believe without proof. We talked on the phone a week later and she could already visualize herself passing. This was a major breakthrough! From that point on I knew she would pass. Her ability to concentrate while studying improved dramatically as her focus shifted from the exam to her successful career selling real estate.

Jerri had developed the confidence necessary to keep her from choking on her real estate exam. From failure, she had acquired faith, and ultimately succeeded.

TOO COOL

Have you ever listened to someone talk as if they were too cool to be bothered with studying, grades, making the team, playing to win, or simply participating in whatever? Unfortunately, we have all encountered such fools. Why am I being so harsh? Because these people have no faith. They can't handle failure. In effect, they are afraid to test their talents.

"What difference does it make?" grumbles Jimmy, a veteran of life at age 19, whose pierced ears, nose, eyebrows, and nipples compliment his multicolored hair and numerous tattoos. "I can't find a job that pays squat, I've got no money, and a piece of junk car, so why not make a statement?" An obvious example of the negative programming cycle, and a complete lack of faith.

If you listened to Jimmy ramble, you would hear him alternate between blaming the government and his parents. Regardless, Jimmy has channeled his frustrations into being cool and making a statement. But not only is there no plan for the future, he has given up on making anything of his life. This is both sad and stupid. If Jimmy could learn how to believe without proof, work towards a meaningful goal, he could enjoy his version of Jerri's success.

The ultimate cop-out in life is to waste away on the sidelines. You know the Monday-morning quarterback who has never played the game but has all the answers.

You find people of this nature of all ages. Accept their talk at face value and they appear to have all the answers. Take a careful look at what they do and you will see a different story, a story whose central character is afraid to put his talents to the test, afraid to challenge himself, and afraid to believe. I don't know Jimmy personally, but the odds are that his nipple-pierced, tattooed statement is an attempt to cover up his fear of putting his talents to the test.

There is a direct connection between the positive programming cycle, being able to believe without proof, and constructive Mind Power. Jerri developed it, Jimmy has yet to even try. You can not have one without the other. If you want to put this to a test, go back to your role model exercise. Were these high achievers able to believe without proof? Did they develop the habit of using their mind constructively? Were they immersed in the positive programming cycle? I'll bet they were all the aforementioned. They were able to make the most out of life. Because they were open-minded and used their talents, they had faith.

You are in the process of using your mind more constructively than 99 percent of the human population. So now it's important to purge yourself of any preconceived notions and keep your mind wide open. It's important to have enough belief in yourself that you can pick yourself up after getting knocked down. You will fail as you succeed in taking control of your life. Mind Power will help pick you up and get you back in the game.

Reflect back for a moment about the last time you struggled with a decision about whether or not to spend extra time preparing for a test. You knew a little advance preparation would pay off come test day, but some internal force derailed you. It seemed to take control of your best intentions, control your thoughts, switch on destructive Mind Power, and send you in the direction of no belief. You simply didn't prepare, rationalized your lack of activity, and underperformed. Can you relate to this scenario? Most students, in some form or another, can. The trick is making certain this remains an isolated incident. A one-off. If it becomes a habit, you will never be able to believe without proof. Ugh!

Sure, you might still get a poor grade even if you study, but it is highly unlikely, especially when you employ the Mind Power techniques and the study and testing tips in the back of the book.

LEARNING TO BELIEVE

What if Jimmy could reverse all that frustration bottled up in making his statement? What if he could transform all that negative energy and get it working for him in taking control of his life? What if he could be as compelled to become a mechanic, computer programmer, disc jockey, whatever . . . and apply the same intensity he has placed towards giving up on life, to making a life? Do you think he would have a chance? You bet he would!

Even if your situation is not as extreme, if you have been harboring negative emotions towards sports, school, your parents, or your future, not only can you totally turn that negativity into positive energy, you also can develop the power of faith. It's the step that follows developing the positive programming cycle. Once you get control of those tapes inside your head, you gotta believe. The objective is to redirect all the power of your mind that was being applied negatively into living your wildest expectations. For students of Mind Power, this becomes as natural as night following day.

Think of your mind as the control center of an internal belief system with limitless power that can serve your every need. It's what makes you human. This is the facility that elevates us above every other creature in this world. Think about it. The mind provides us with the ability to think, reason, create, dream, believe without proof, and be the dominant force on our planet. This is a bit of a worry, I know. It is an awesome responsibility!

But this is old news. Aristotle (check the *Dictionary of Cultural Literacy* if you don't know who he is) considered the mind as something related to the heart. Plato thought it aligned to the brain. In 1981, Dr. Roger Sperry, a psychobiologist at the California Institute of Technology, won a Nobel Prize in Physiology and Medicine for his work on the functioning of the two hemispheres of the brain. Since then, this has been referred to as split-brain research.

Dr. Sperry proved that we have a left and a right brain that are connected by an elaborate communications network called the corpus callosum. His research informed us that each hemisphere controlled different activities: analytical thinking with the left, creativity and intuition with the right.

Our power to believe without proof stems from the fact our brain and mind are inextricably linked—much like the relationship between the heart and soul. Scientists speak with authority when discussing both the brain and the heart. These are actual organs that they can experiment with and study in their laboratories. For instance, we know the average brain weighs a little over three pounds and has more storage capacity than the largest computer ever built.

Get this, experts tell us that the typical brain, your brain, can store up to two quintillion bits of information. How are you with numbers? That's a two followed by 18 zeros! Ivan Yefremov, a brain specialist from the former Soviet Union, claims that the average person has enough brain power to master 40 languages, memorize a complete set of encyclopedias, and complete the graduation requirements of a dozen universities. Wow! But something is missing here. . . .

With all this alleged brain power, nobody has seen the

mind. One might think that some of that natural intellect would help define something as important as the mind. Though everyone agrees that even the most brilliant human beings use only a fraction of their mental powers, yet every day you are likely to use some of this hidden power without realizing it.

PLAYING A HUNCH

Have you ever played a hunch? You know, used your intuition to assist you in making an important decision. Sure you have. Most people can recall numerous instances. On the other hand, can you remember a time when your intuition failed you? If you think long enough, I'm sure you can. It's that hunch telling you not to trust this new kid in class, the one who ends up becoming a good friend. It's intuition mind power that acts like a spiritual consciousness. Some people call it psychic energy. It doesn't matter, the label is not important. What is important is that you understand the totality of Mind Power, as well as its fallibility. As your intuition testifies, however accurate, it's not infallible, but the more you use it the more accurate it becomes.

"Hold on. Slow down," you're saying. "All I want to do is get 1150 on my SAT, and maybe start working on my other goals." Okay. Hang on and allow me to give two simple illustrations that help clarify what I'm talking about, and demonstrate how natural, and powerful, these powers of the mind really are in everyday life. This should also give you an understanding how you can exercise your intuition. One illustration will be constructive, the other . . .

Constructive Mind Power: Imagine yourself preparing to go away for a three-day weekend at the beach with your best friends. You're psyched! It's a six-hour drive and you're being picked up at 6 A.M., but you're up late talking on the phone and arranging last-minute details. Because of the early hour, you ask your mother to awaken you at 5 A.M.; in addition, you set your own alarm clock.

As you fall asleep your mind is already at the beach. You see yourself lying in the sun with your friends and you know you must get up at 5 A.M. At 4:59 A.M. a miracle happens, you wake up before your mother and the alarm. The natural alarm clock in your mind took care of business. Has this ever happened to you?

Destructive Mind Power: Picture yourself preparing to deliver an oral presentation on the Civil War to your entire history class. Your teacher is not only tough, you think he's mean. You know you're going to look like a fool and embarrass yourself—you're worried. You go to bed early, worrying about this teacher and the questions he will ask. You then have trouble sleeping, you forget to set your alarm, you oversleep and spend the rest of the morning trying to convince your mother you are too sick to go to school. Have you ever been there?

As I have stated repeatedly, Mind Power is either constructive or destructive. It doesn't perform halfway. When Jerri switched her constructive Mind Power switch, she took control of her life. Jimmy's switch is still locked on destructive. The amazing thing about Mind Power is the ease with which anyone can flip the switch to constructive. Anyone can routinely program their subconscious to awaken them in the morning, much like any student can program an illness to avoid a difficult situation. Could you imagine Columbus calling in sick when he realized he had not reached Eastern Asia?

In both instances, Mind Power was involved without any real conscious effort. You, my friend, hold the key to your mental switch. Whenever you have any questions about this mental switch, reread the section about garbage in/garbage out in Chapter 2. Just imagine the power at your fingertips when you make a habit of channeling all of this power towards your Master Dream List.

But to believe without proof requires faith. Faith is what provides the strength to keep going when the going gets tough. And it will and so will you. In the next chapter, as promised, I am going to take you through the Achievement Cycle in great detail. You are already in it, but you are ready for a more thorough understanding.

WRAP-UP

- You gotta believe without proof.
- Faith provides the strength to overcome failure.
- You must fail to succeed.
- The original sin is not using your God-given talents.
- Mind Power is nondenominational.
- Learn a lesson from the professor and the Zen Master.
- Your mind places you above every other creature on the planet.
- Mind Power is either constructive or destructive.
- Control your mental switch and you control your life.

Chapter 11

The Cycle of Achievement

"You make up your mind before you start that sacrifice is part of the package."
—Richard M. DeVos

Can you recall public enemy number 1? That negative programming cycle that has been replaced with the number 1 success habit: the positive programming cycle. Sure you remember, because every time you listen to your affirmation tape you are reinforcing your success habit. But I want to take you a step further in understanding the process of achievement—or, should I say, the psychology of achievement.

Get ready for more action. Everything you have learned thus far about Mind Power will become even more useful once you have a thorough understanding of the basic laws of achievement. Most people have a vague understanding of the conscious and subconscious mind. Your affirmation tape, mental signal, and goal-getting exercise have provided you with a strong working knowledge. In this chapter I am going to take that working knowledge to a higher level.

First, a little background on the mind. Many experts like to place percentages on these two components of the mind, usually allotting 90 percent or more of our latent mental power to the subconscious. I agree. It's like a huge untapped gold mine. Our conscious mind is thought to be much smaller, less than 10 percent. These figures are not important; it's your understanding of the specific roles they each play in the cycle of achievement that will enable you to become a true master of Mind Power.

THE CONSCIOUS MIND

This is our thinking mind. It harbors either the negative or positive programming cycle and provides us with the ability to rationalize and reason. This is the facility that enables students, and adults, to create elaborate excuses for not turning in their homework assignments on time. Or blame a teacher for a poor grade. Though considered less than 10 percent of our mental power, it is the key to all of our power. For instance, it was your conscious mind that programmed you to wake up at 4:59 A.M. for that weekend with your friends.

Likewise, it was your conscious mind that played tricks on you when it came to that oral presentation. Your conscious thoughts programmed that high anxiety. By dwelling on negative thoughts, public enemy number 1 and corresponding programming entered into your subconscious mind. Oversleeping was your subconscious cop-out, your sudden illness was your conscious mind trying to rationalize your cop-out. Not an effective strategy. Then again, destructive Mind Power never is.

Both your parents and teachers condition you to think. They focus on your conscious thoughts and teach you to use your conscious mind with little consideration provided to the subconscious. So much emphasis is placed on thinking that many students get headaches from thinking too much. Adults suffer also. Too much thinking leads to negative thinking, which causes worry, and worry acts as a cancer to productive behavior. The irony is that we are taught to remember, pay attention, analyze, be logical, use deductive reasoning, and are rewarded for mastery of such conscious skills. Students who can memorize facts usually get good grades.

Fortunately, or maybe unfortunately, the skills that help a student get good grades in the classroom are not always the same skills that lead a person to live up to his/her wildest expectations. This is why some good students never seem to take control of their lives and fail to live up to those glorified expectations. Yet I have seen below-average students achieve far beyond anyone's wildest anticipation. What gives?

As a child, you were taught to expect success through stubbing your toes and skinning your knees. Nobody ever learned how to ride a bicycle without falling. This is a paradox that many adults have forgotten and too many school systems are unequipped to deal with. Students need to believe in themselves, recognize they are born to achieve, but they must also understand the inner workings of the Cycle of Achievement. From my vantage point, it's hard for parents and teachers to teach what they don't understand. You'll get a chuckle out of this anonymous quote from the nineteenth century, as it sums up a situation that hasn't changed as we get ready for the twenty-first century: "We know more about breeding high grades of cattle than we do about developing high-quality adults." You won't get much argument from me.

CONSCIOUS THOUGHTS

If you have recorded your affirmation tape and begun using it, you are taking control of your conscious thoughts by developing the number 1 success habit, the positive programming cycle. As you know, every conscious thought sends a programming message to your subconscious mind. Those thoughts that are repeated over and over determine your automatic behavior. They become the recorded tapes that play in your head. You are rerecording these tapes to your likeness—which means, you are taking control of the foundation for all habits, good and bad.

Nerves that interfere with getting a good test score are the result of the bad habit of worrying about the exam, exactly the same as nerves that cause a missed free throw with the game on the line. Both are the result of the conscious mind. Victor Frankel, an Austrian psychiatrist who lived through Hitler's prison camps, referred to this as anticipatory anxiety—a dysfunctional use of the conscious mind. Unfortunately, it often becomes a habit.

Nothing is more destructive to a student, or any human being for that matter, than to become dysfunctional with conscious thoughts. You name the fear, and the odds are that it was developed over time through repeated thoughts. Fear of tests, public speaking, fear of failure, fear of success, and low self-esteem are all products of public enemy number 1: the negative programming cycle. Thus is the ongoing power of the conscious mind.

Bob was the captain of his golf team and considered one of the top golfers in his conference. He had a natural swing, good concentration, and a great short game—except, that is, under pressure. He was so good that rarely was an opponent able to push him. This is why Bob was able to ignore his problem for as long as he did.

Nobody knew Bob's thoughts prior to and during a competitive match. But his thoughts were anything but positive, ''I hope this guy's no good. I hope this isn't a close match. I hope I don't blow it,'' and so on. His talent let him get away with such garbage-in until a regional tournament where there were other golfers who could push him.

That's all it took. Bob's conscious mind took over and fed him a steady diet of negative thoughts. He played horribly on every back nine and scored poorly throughout the tournament. Because his programming was so flawed, he didn't have a chance. Each round got worse, to the extent he almost defaulted the last day because of sickness. Fortunately, he avoided being labeled a quitter. Bob was sick only in the head, and everyone knew it. Only following such a humiliating experience was Bob able to recognize the role his mind played in his achievements.

Your basic understanding of how your conscious mind programs your subconscious is going to enable you to master the Cycle of Achievement. The reason I've had you actively reprogramming the tapes in your head by listening to your affirmation tape is because positive thoughts on top of negative programming only creates tension. Tension always seeks a release, and therefore the tendency is to revert back to your old prerecorded programming. Bob, for instance, needed to work on his reprogramming before the tournament.

If we agree that the human brain is the world's most powerful computer, you can follow my reasoning when I claim that the conscious mind is the most skilled computer programmer. You receive information—"math is a killer," you reason, "nobody's ever gotten an A so there's no point in working too hard"—and you act—you do as little as possible to get by. As with any computer, this entire scenario could just as easily be reversed by changing the programming input to positive information, creating reason to believe you could get an A, and you then give it your best effort.

The conscious mind dictates your input and ultimately the corresponding action. Dwelling on negative information leads to rationalization and improper, if any, activity. When the focus is on positive input the reverse occurs. Although the conscious mind represents only 5 to 10 percent of our Mind Power, it is easy to recognize the importance of the role it plays. The conscious mind thinks. The thoughts we dwell on are what determines our automatic behavior. They are what programs our subconscious minds. Your affirmation tape is actually serving a dual purpose; it helps reprogram your subconscious mind, and it assists in developing the habit of turning thoughts into affirmation statements.

Bob couldn't avoid choking during the most critical golf tournament of his high school career. He was programmed to choke in the midst of tough competition, which is exactly what he did.

Whenever you think of Mind Power, think of your conscious mind as your center of reason. It has the ability to make choices. You can choose to dwell on thoughts that make you angry or thoughts that stimulate positive emotions. You can choose to study after school with your Dream Team Buddy, or alone at night. You can decide whether you are going to be courteous or discourteous to your parents. You have created a Master Dream List. All these decisions, every decision, is made with your conscious mind.

Where the problem lies with this conscious power to choose is when you rationalize negative behavior. There are too many excuses, and many students have taken excuses to an art form. Whenever you hear an excuse, yours or someone else's, you are witnessing destructive Mind Power. Think about it.

THE CYCLE OF ACHIEVEMENT

In the Cycle of Achievement, your conscious mind is the vehicle that puts you in motion. It creates action. I refer to this as your DOING state. You have direct control over this component of the cycle. Consider the following:

THE CYCLE OF ACHIEVEMENT

Goal
↓
Doing

Thinking

↓

Feeling

↓

Goal/Goal Accomplishment

There is a bit of the proverbial "What came first, the chicken or the egg?" question with regard to doing and thinking, thinking and doing. But when you consider both ease and control over the desired outcome, it's easier to understand my emphasis on doing—activity, regardless of what you think at the time, or how you feel.

For instance, follow my instructions and determine which was the easiest to execute. Let's start with trying to control your feelings. At the end of this sentence, stop reading for a moment and conjure up the feeling of fear. Go ahead, give it a whirl. For most people this is a difficult request. There is nothing to make you fearful while reading these lines. Now after reading this sentence, think about your left foot. No big deal, just think about it. It's easier than trying to feel fear, but you still must concentrate. Right? If not, your mind will wander. Now let's get into doing, an activity. Raise your left hand. Just do it.

DOING

Okay. Hopefully I have made my point. DOING—walking, talking, writing your Master Dream List, studying, listening to your affirmation tape . . . these are acts—DO's—which involve your conscious mind making a decision to act. For the most part, you have complete control over this component of the Cycle of Achievement. Consider this the action phase of the cycle. The bonus is that the action phase dictates the remaining components. Reading this book is an act. Hanging out at the mall is an act. Talking with your Dream Team Buddy is an act. Synergistic goal-getting is an act.

The secret is linking your activities to a specific goal, a dream. You have already done this and are currently working towards living up to your wildest expectations. This is precisely what your fixed daily activities are all about. Activity that is not linked can cause problems. Why? Because activity impacts how we think and feel. It can help accelerate constructive thinking and good feelings or it can fuel the opposite. So once the goal is established, an act that requires thinking and doing, always remember the following:

Action linked to goals cures fear.
Action linked to goals builds confidence and self-esteem.
Action linked to goals produces achievement.

THINKING

The act of making and listening to your affirmation tape has a direct impact on your thinking. You have both voluntary and involuntary thoughts. As in the case of Bob, when it came to playing golf under pressure, his involuntary thoughts were self-limiting. They interfered with his action on the golf course. Shortly after his poor tournament showing, by adding an action, DOING, before he found himself under such pressure again, he was able to get control over those involuntary thoughts. The combination of affirmation tape, synergistic goal-getting exercise, control flame, and a specific pre-shot routine while actually playing golf enabled Bob to control his involuntary thoughts. He no longer chokes.

But in order to change, be it Bob on the golf course or you taking a test, you typically are required to act in a fashion that is uncomfortable. This is good! It's usually uncomfortable for most people to make an affirmation tape. And, at first, it's equally awkward listening to your voice. But you do it anyway. This gives you the element of control over those involuntary thoughts of your subconscious, and then you begin the process of impacting your feelings.

FEELINGS

For some people feelings are a blessing, for others they are a curse. Feelings. We all have them, and most people are controlled by them. Their loss. Actually one of the blessings we have as a species is such a wide range of feelings: happiness, love, joy, anger, anxiety, fear, excitement, nervousness, motivation, laziness. Too many people, students and adults alike, have turned this blessing into a curse. They feel totally driven. All behavior is determined by how they feel. If they feel like studying, they study. If they feel like exercising, they work out. If they don't, you guessed it. . . .

Your feelings are deep-seated within you. They are the result of years of involuntary thoughts as your subconscious mind is basically playing the program that you have recorded. Years of telling yourself things like, "I'm no good," "It's no use," "I'm not good with numbers," "I test poorly," have impacted your feelings of today. Do you know anyone who always seems to be up and another who always appears to be down? One person is in control, the other is not.

Doing your fixed daily activities linked to your goal, doing your goal-getting exercise, listening to your affirmation tape . . . enables you to change all of this subconscious programming. Gone is that involuntary self-limiting thinking. Gone is that feeling of jealousy. Gone is that feeling of apathy that has kept you from acting on your best intentions. Gone is your number 1 bad habit, or what I also refer to as public enemy number 1.

You are now in play, fully engaged in the Cycle of Achievement—doing those fixed daily activities, which impact your thinking and build confidence, which in turn impact how you feel about yourself and boost self-esteem, which ultimately lead you to your accomplishment. Wow. What a cycle!

YOUR SUBCONSCIOUS MIND

Welcome to the epicenter of all your emotions, all of your habits, and all of your involuntary behavior. No wonder it's designated 90-plus percent of your total Mind Power. This is your creative mind. Here is where you are intuitive, where your conscious message to awaken yourself at 4:59 A.M. is actually programmed, where those hunches come from. In contrast to your conscious mind, which is considered to be rational, your subconscious functions almost on an irrational level.

I touched on some of these concepts when instructing you in making your affirmation tape. But this is important enough to warrant a little repetition. What is important to realize about your subconscious is that its strength is also a weakness. This powerful entity, the source of all your programming, cannot distinguish between fact and fiction. How's that for being irrational? It simply accepts every repeated thought as fact—hence the value of listening to your affirmation tape, thank you very much. This omnipotent force of nature, representing in excess of 90 percent of your Mind Power, plays second fiddle to your conscious thoughts. It's hostage. This is why most people go through life hostage to their internal programming.

This is only a problem for the uninitiated, those poor fools who think they're only being realistic when they repeat, to anyone who will listen, statements like ''I hate homework." It's the repetition of such unhealthy messages that causes problems. Take studying, for example. Most students would rather do something else, anything, rather than study. Right? Just as every student recognizes that studying is a requirement linked to learning, especially in school. The problem is that most students are not very efficient at studying.

Many students spend too much time studying because they have trouble concentrating. This failure to concentrate interferes with their ability to absorb knowledge and forces them to spend more time at the books only to get sub-par results. There is no rational basis for this. One would think students would have figured out how to study in the most time-efficient manner long ago. But this irrational, inefficient, and ineffective behavior is merely a function of subconscious programming. Have you ever wasted a lot of time studying only to get a poor result?

THE SUBCONSCIOUS GARDEN

By this juncture you're familiar with all the parallels between computers and the mind. Terms such as programming, reprogramming, garbage-in/garbage-out, and others have become interchangeable. Prior to all this computer jargon, the subconscious was often equated with a garden. If you have ever planted a garden, or helped one of your parents weed their vegetable garden, you know the soil does not discriminate between the vegetable seeds and the weeds. Oh how I hated helping my father weed his vegetable garden!

The soil accepts any seed, good or bad. In fact, if you're not careful with your garden, weeds tend to dominate. I remember returning from a two-week family vacation and looking forward to playing with my friends, only to see a garden full of weeds that had to be attended to. Your mind functions in much the same way. Your thoughts are the seeds, your subconscious mind your garden. Like your garden, your subconscious mind has two characteristics in common: first, your subconscious accepts every seed (thought) as an equal; second, if left unattended weeds dominate (negative programming).

Both of these commonalties are critical in your understanding of Mind Power. If you stop listening to your affirmation tape or stray away from your goal-getting exercise, picture a vegetable garden left untended for three weeks. The weeds wouldn't have taken over completely, but they would have made a mess. Similarly, you won't have completely lost touch with your Master Dream List, but you would slip back into some old bad habits. And that's messy.

Beware. There is a strong tendency to revert back to old habits once a goal is achieved. I have seen students and adults both fall into this trap. After seemingly mastering the powers of the mind and getting their immediate goals, they stop the exact activities that drove the process. Almost like killing the goose that laid the golden egg, the tendency is to get a bit lazy and stop using the Mind Power techniques. Your Mind Power exercises are akin to your push-ups, sit-ups, an early-morning run—you have to do them regularly if you want to stay in shape. Mental shape.

Equally important is remembering that your subconscious mind is incapable of determining the accuracy of your thoughts. It has no idea if the message you send is true or false, good or bad, constructive or destructive. As you have learned by using your affirmation tape, your subconscious responds to whatever thoughts you repeat over and over and over. These are the seeds you plant. It's through constant attention to this programming that you become the master of your subconscious. All of this tends to seem a bit theoretical, but it's actually a DOING component of your Cycle of Achievement. The importance of being proactive with activities within your control cannot be emphasized enough!

THE POWER OF SUGGESTION

All human beings are vulnerable to the power of suggestion. You, your teachers, and parents, and every one of your friends. Whether it's weakening to peer pressure and skipping class, youngsters watching violence on television, or your mother trying to recapture her youth with a new convertible—nobody is immune to the power of suggestion. Why? Because our subconscious mind accepts all sensory input, and suggestions are sensory input. If the sensory input happens to coincide with existing programming, the impact can be immediate. When students have been programmed that they are never going to amount to much in life, skipping class is a simple decision. A four-year-old boy who has been fed a steady diet of television programs illustrating violence as the means for solving conflict is more likely to hit than talk. And the beat goes on.

RECOGNIZING THE NEGATIVES

Most students have experienced the power of classic negative programming regarding courses and teachers. It's a new school year and you have been assigned to Mr. Snider for Language Arts class. His reputation precedes him—he is the toughest teacher in the school. He will work you to death. He is very strict. Expect tons of homework. And before you walk into Mr. Snider's classroom the first time, you're thinking of ways to transfer out of his class. You and every other student.

Although you have never had an interaction with Mr. Snider, you have this bad feeling about him. You don't like him.

Because you are being driven by your feelings in this scenario, feelings that have been caused by negative programming, your objectivity has disappeared. Rather than beginning this class with your typical goal of getting an A, taking time to understand the teacher and what he wants, and then developing your strategy accordingly, you've done nothing. You have given in to your feelings.

By being able to recognize negative programming signals and using your control flame, you can remain in control and doing. In this instance, you would recognize the reputation of Mr. Snider but would not dwell on it. Whenever you would find anxiety about him entering your mind, you would simply visualize your control flame, take a belly breath, and repeat an affirmation statement to yourself: "I get an A in Language Arts," or "I enjoy Mr. Snider's class," or whatever. The secret is recognition and appropriate action.

POSITIVE PROGRAMMING

For every Mr. Snider there is a Ms. Bell. She is the science teacher everyone loves. It's not that she's an easy mark, because she isn't. It's her personality, the way she involves the class in experiments, and her creativity in assignments. Ms. Bell has a reputation for making learning science fun. And you have been assigned to Ms. Bell's science class.

You're elated. You can't wait to meet this teacher everybody loves. You are determined to get an A, you're excited about figuring out what she wants, and creating a strategy to make certain you get your goal.

You are immersed in activity. Because the programming is positive, your feelings are positive and are engaged in action. The problem is that most people can be fair-weather achievers and learn well from a Ms. Bell. Unfortunately, not everyone is a Ms. Bell. There are plenty of Mr. Sniders who test your resolve. Think of Mr. Snider as a symbol for the negative: an obstacle, a challenge, bad feelings. Let Ms. Bell be a symbol for the positive: smooth sailing, good feelings. You need to be able to handle both.

Goal-getting action is what will carry you through. You appreciate the Ms. Bells in life, and work through the Mr. Sniders by staying on course with your fixed daily activities and Mind Power exercises. Sure it might be harder to get an A in Mr. Snider's class, but you probably were forced to exercise more of your Mind Power.

No suggestion can be acted upon by a subconscious that is in conflict with your conscious mind. Your conscious mind is your filtering device. You hear all the gossip about Mr. Snider, but you reject it as inappropriate programming and move forward towards your goal. The mind of a goal-getter is constantly rejecting negative messages aimed to interfere with achievement.

Average students struggle because they develop a habit of allowing negative messages entrance into that fertile soil of the subconscious. Without realizing it, they develop the habit of focusing on problems and being driven through life by their feelings and never benefit from the Cycle of Achievement—goal focus–doing–thinking–feeling.

THE RETICULAR ACTIVATING SYSTEM

With the risk of getting too technical, I am going to describe a subconscious filtering system that might help clarify everything you already know about Mind Power. Each of us is armed with a netlike group of cells at the base of our brain. Neuroscientists call this device the *reticular activating system*. It screens every message that passes through your brain every day. That's thousands of messages. It sends through to your cerebral cortex only those messages deemed important.

Because your brain has the capability of being aware of every form of sensory stimuli, you would quickly have sensory overload without this screening mechanism. The reticular activating system screens out all messages except for those that are of two types: messages of value and messages that are threatening. Think of it in terms of having two automatic antennas, one over each ear. Whenever there is a fearful message, the fear antenna pops up over your left ear and attracts all pertinent information associated with that particular fear. A value message causes the value antenna to surface above your right ear and attract information considered to be of value. This is where it gets both interesting and useful for you.

VALUE ANTENNA

Can you remember the last time you had a crush on someone? You caught a glimpse of that new girl in your study hall. Instinctively your value antenna goes up. Within a short period of time you know everything about this new girl. You know her class schedule, where she lives, the car her parents drive—you know everything. Why? Because your reticular activating system was responding to a value message. You had a crush on this girl.

Goals manipulate your reticular activating system in a similar manner. Your value antenna goes out for any type of information that will assist you in achieving your goal. Which is why it is important to both write and visualize your goals. You want that value antenna out as much as possible.

FEAR ANTENNA

Think of the last time you worried about a test. What happened was that your mind interpreted your worry as fear and activated your fear antenna. Your fear antenna went up! I know, it sounds foolish, but that is exactly what happened. This fear antenna then acted like a magnet, sucking in all information to feed your worries concerning this test. You knew other people who had failed. You couldn't concentrate as well as you wanted when studying. You knew you wouldn't be able to recall all the information. And guess what? You didn't.

The only thing you want to use your fear antenna for is emergencies. Think of it as only a fight-or-flight device. You smell smoke, your fear antenna goes up and takes in all the information about a possible fire. Is there a fire? Where are the exits? Is there a fire extinguisher? Where is the phone to call the fire department? Use it any other way and it will derail you from achieving your goals.

Again the important thing is developing the habit of using your mind constructively. This is how you get lucky. That good old value antenna is consistently working to gather information to assist you in reaching your goals, to living up to your wildest expectations. Every time you reread your Master Dream List you activate your value antenna. Understanding how these antennas function will help you in everything you do. Using your value antenna is a DO.

As you learn how to keep that value antenna fully engaged, it's helpful to have a good working knowledge of what is referred to as ''attitude.'' As you read the next chapter, ''Maintaining a Winning Attitude,'' think of the adults you know and their attitudes.

WRAP-UP

- Your conscious mind enables you to rationalize.
- Your subconscious mind is irrational and doesn't know the difference between fact and fiction.
- The conscious mind programs the subconscious.
- The Cycle of Achievement: goal–doing–thinking–feeling–goal accomplishment.
- Activity drives the dream: DO!
- Your subconscious mind is like a garden, very susceptible to programming.
- The reticular activating system screens all sensory input.
- You have two antennas: fear and value.
- Goals manipulate your value antenna.

Chapter 12

Maintaining a Winning Attitude

"It has been my observation that people are just about as happy as they make up their minds to be."

—Abraham Lincoln

If you have a Dream Team Buddy, I want you to meet with him/her and take inventory of both of your attitudes. The odds are that you know of someone who is down, miserable, or outright depressed. Unfortunately, too many students suffer from such attitudinal swings without appearing to have any control over them. They are completely vulnerable to moods. This is not something simply accompanying adolescence. It's a sign of the pressures students feel in today's world and it affects adults as well—this seeming lack of control over our attitude.

Yesterday an incident happened at my swim and tennis club that illustrates what I am talking about. I had taken my oldest daughter, Heidi, and five-year-old son Patrick to the club. Patrick was hanging out with RJ, the pro's seven-year-old son, waiting for me to take him into the pool after I finished a few tennis drills with Heidi. All was well until RJ went home with his father. Patrick came slowly walking onto our tennis court holding his head.

Heidi told him to get off the court. I assured him that we were almost finished but also asked him to get off the court. He kept walking, on the court, directly towards me holding his head. Heidi wasn't too pleased and told Patrick so. He ignored her completely and he was now standing directly in front of me.

As soon as we made direct eye contact, he began crying and told me how he fell and hit his head on a wheelbarrow. He did have a huge bump on his head, so it was obvious he had banged into something, yet he had delayed crying until RJ had gone home. He controlled his attitude. He was not going to cry in front of his older friend. A few minutes, a bit of reassurance, and a turn at hitting a handful of tennis balls and all was forgotten, until we got home and Patrick saw his mother. Minus the tears, he recounted his problem with the wheelbarrow once again.

This scene is repeated in every household, every day. Children consciously choose their attitude. Whether they get a bump on the head, fall off a bike, or are told to clean their room, depending on various external circumstances, an appropriate response is chosen. Recently Amy, my 10-year-old daughter, was in a funk at the dinner table because her mother had reminded her that it was her turn to do the dishes. This caused a loose tooth she had been monitoring to hurt, which hindered her eating, prompted my teasing, and left Amy sitting alone at the table with a look of total depression—until one of her friends telephoned. Then she flipped her switch and choose a good attitude.

The secret is being able to recognize and control your attitude without the need for external interference. Nothing is more important in your ability to capitalize on your resources than your attitude. I have seen teenagers with such bad attitudes that it was obvious they had learned this behavior at a young age and had no idea how to control it. This is unfortunate.

Sadly, parents with terrible attitudes often have a direct impact on their children. If you are caught in this predicament, you don't need to rush off and trade in your parents. But you do need to recognize that attitude is a learned behavior. And you must pay close attention to controlling your attitude. The worst part of what I see in bad-attitude students is the accompanying underachievement, which fuels their bad attitude. And this seemingly vicious cycle is so unnecessary. For the most part, people with bad attitudes can change as long as they are not like the proverbial ostrich with its head buried in the sand, refusing to accept that their attitude is holding them back.

Whenever the topic of attitude comes up I am reminded of a tale about a teacher who offered his students a prize of $500 for the best thought. The money was awarded to a student for the following submission: "Men grumble because God put thorns with roses; wouldn't it be better to thank God for putting roses with thorns?" What kind of attitude do you think that student possessed? Even more positive after receiving the $500 prize, I know.

It's always easy to make sense of these issues when reading a book or listening to someone talk; the challenge always surfaces when dealing with life. Roses and thorns have been a prickly issue for me, no pun intended, for a long time. My wife loves rosesbushes and has them well situated throughout our yard. Because she gives them tender loving care they grow rapidly and aggressively. My challenge is mowing the lawn without getting bloodied. And, I must confess, each scratch takes a bite out of my healthy attitude to the extent that on one occasion I was foolish enough grab this thorny branch and attempt to snap it, only to bloody my hand. Dumb squared! My attitude then took a turn south, as my wife watched my display of temper, and the rosebush was still alive and well.

As much as we work at controlling our mind and striving to live our wildest expectations, we must always pay close attention to our attitude. Everybody is vulnerable to copping an attitude, and it's usually a bad attitude that is copped. Whether it's losing one's temper, being overly critical, obnoxious, negative, or outright destructive, many people have a blind spot when it comes to their attitude. Oh, sure, they can spot a bad attitude in someone else a mile away, but when it comes to looking in the mirror. . . .

Take a moment, right now, to reflect back to the last time you copped a bad attitude, got down on yourself, or began complaining about things. Was it productive? How does the memory sit with you now? Most people are embarrassed by such honest recollections. I know I am. But now picture yourself in the same situation taking control of your attitude. The immediate outcome might not change dramatically—Patrick still had a lump on his head, Amy still had to wash the dishes—but whenever you control your attitude in the midst of adversity, a surge of inner strength comes over you. You have elevated yourself above the masses. You know you could have snapped but you took control instead. You will always feel better when taking control over your attitude. This is the essence of Mind Power.

In taking control of your life, developing the habit of functioning in the positive programming cycle, make certain that neither you nor your Dream Team Buddy have any blind spots when it comes to attitude. It's not that you can never have a bad mood, it's just that you do not want to be either helpless or blind to these shifts in attitude. The simplest method I have discovered for accomplishing this is having a heart-to-heart talk with your Dream Team Buddy or someone else you trust.

Discuss what other people think of the old you, prior to your involvement with Mind Power. Do you agree with those assessments? How do you view your old self? Look for both consistencies and inconsistencies. Do not look for idle flattery, it will get you nowhere. Then discuss the changes you have made since applying these Mind Power principles. Are they noticeable? Are other people recognizing them? Where do you notice the biggest change? Discuss these questions, add some of your own, and complete the following Winning Attitude Profile. It will assist you in this exercise as it provides a degree of structure for both of you to begin with.

WAP: WINNING ATTITUDE PROFILE

	Strongly Agree	Mildly Agree	Mildly Disagree	Strongly Disagree
1. I tend to blame other people for my problems.	4	3	2	1
2. I always wonder what other people think of me.	4	3	2	1
3. I have yet to really commit myself to my talents.	4	3	2	1
4. I tend to dwell on mistakes.	4	3	2	1
5. I feel tremendous pressure to perform.	4	3	2	1
6. I have trouble sticking to my study schedule.	4	3	2	1
7. I have trouble believing I am good enough.	4	3	2	1
8. I take criticism personally.	4	3	2	1
9. I look for the best in others.	1	2	3	4
10. I avoid negative people.	1	2	3	4

11. I find myself listening to and spreading gossip.	4	3	2	1
12. I am highly critical of my parents and teachers when talking with friends.	4	3	2	1
13. I stick up for people who are being picked on.	1	2	3	4
14. I recognize my down moods and pull myself up.	1	2	3	4
15. I enjoy people.	1	2	3	4

Scoring the Winning Attitude Profile: You will determine your WAP score by adding all the numbers you circled.

Maximum Score = 60   My Score_____

Score:

60–53   You better make working to improve your attitude a fixed daily activity. Develop a checklist with your Dream Team Buddy. Work on one or two areas at a time. Understand that your attitude can hold you back *big time*!

52–45   You have some work to do, keep on top of your Mind Power exercises and you will make major strides in developing your attitude. Make it a top priority.

44–36   Average student attitude. It is holding you back in a typical manner. Recognize your strengths and weaknesses and work on them.

35–21   Your attitude is a major strength. With a little
         work you will be in complete control over
         your destiny. Make certain your buddy has an
         equally strong attitude.
20–15   Contact me! You can assist me with me oc-
         casional lapses in attitude. Your potential is
         unlimited!

After you have finished this profile with your Dream
Team Buddy and have come to terms with the assessment
of you attitude, make a commitment to correct one weakness every week. It's your attitude, not your aptitude, that
will determine how much you achieve on your Master
Dream List. Commit with your buddy to develop the habit
of being confident, good-natured, caring, courageous, and
sharing. How's that for personal qualities?

You want to be that breath of fresh air, that ray of
sunshine, wherever you go, to whomever you encounter.
The benefits are beyond description, but you will enjoy
better health and cheer in everything you do.

On the flip side, avoid bad-attitude people like the
plague. These people are poison! Attitudes are contagious
and you want to be a carrier of good not a receiver of
bad. A depressed, down attitude will bring you down,
whether you realize it or not. It's the law of attraction.
Sure, you might be able to bring the other person up, but
be careful how much energy you expend on these people.
The best advice is to stay away from them.

Many variables impact the attitudes of today's students.
With almost half of all marriages ending in divorce and
a growing number of children being raised in single-
parent homes, attitudes are being shaped under less than
favorable conditions. Add the stress placed on grades and
negative peer pressure to get involved in destructive activities such as alcohol and drug abuse, and it's important

to constantly use your Mind Power tools to stay on top of your attitude.

Enthusiasm can make you healthy, while worry can make you sick. Either way, the physical state is controlled by the mental frame of mind—attitude. As you continue your journey through life, working to live your wildest expectations, the following list of 24 personality characteristics might be helpful to keeping that winning attitude. This list is is far from complete, but it can point you in the right direction.

Friendly	Patient	Understanding	Fair
Benevolent	Sober	Gentle	Peaceful
Honest	Tolerant	Listening	Value-based
Humble	Courteous	Dependable	God-loving
Enthusiastic	Loving	Clean	Family-focused
Kind	Humorous	Poised	Decisive
Loyal	Tactful	Charitable	Brave

As you add to this list with qualities you consider in keeping with maintaining a winning attitude, it's helpful to recall one of Confucius' pearls of wisdom: "Behave towards everyone as if receiving a guest."

WRAP-UP

- Your attitude will determine your life's journey.
- Attitude is far more important than aptitude in working your Master Dream List.
- Beware of attitudinal blind spots.
- You are in control of your attitude.
- Work with your buddy on attitude development.
- "Know thyself"—Socrates.

Chapter 13

Self-Esteem in Action

"Many receive advice, only the wise profit from it."

—Syrus

If you have heard it once, you have heard it in some form or another at least one thousand times: "You need high self-esteem in order to succeed." This is one of the reasons so few people get so little out of life. Not because they have low self-esteem, but because they are waiting to increase their self-esteem in order to achieve. Actually it has become quite popular for both parents and educators to focus on how students feel.

Let me give you an example. Herk DeGraw is a friend of mine who also happens to be one of the best high-school soccer coaches in North Carolina, winning the state tournament a number of times. According to Herk, there is ongoing pressure from parents about their children making the team and getting more playing time. Parents have also complained about his discipline—kids who goof off in practice are made to run laps after practice. Apparently this is too strict in the eyes of some parents.

Because of his success, Herk has been able to create ground rules with the backing of his principal that buffer him from such interference, but it seems that parents think if their Mary doesn't feel like practicing hard, she doesn't have to.

It appears that too many people are concerned with how

people feel, rather than what they do. Sure feelings are hurt whenever someone gets cut from the soccer team, or any team for that matter. I remember clearly the day I got cut from the high school basketball team. It was not a pleasant experience, but I recovered. I realized that I was never going to be much of a basketball player and I went on to become a good wrestler.

The idea that you need high self-esteem to achieve, that you must feel good about yourself to succeed, is pure rubbish. It is something that has been promoted by self-professed self-esteem experts peddling their wares. Why do people buy it? Because so few people are true achievers. They simply do not know the truth about achievement.

What the world needs is more tough love. When a teacher asks you to rewrite a term paper because you used the wrong format, rewrite the paper. Do you have to feel good about it? Of course not! When my wrestling coach caught me fooling around in practice and penalized me by making me wrestle two heavier teammates, back to back, I was not a happy camper. Did I complain to my mother? Not on your life! I wrestled my butt off, crawled out of practice, and vowed never to get caught fooling around again. Ha, the operative word being "caught."

The real question you must ask is, "Am I tough enough?" Are you tough enough to take the necessary action that will build your self-esteem? Are you tough enough to get mad when you fail and take action to do something constructive about it? People who can only handle success and praise will always have problems with self-esteem.

There is no way you should feel good about getting an F on an exam. There was no way I could feel good when I got pinned in a collegiate wrestling tournament. But those feelings must be transferred into corrective action in order to strengthen self-esteem. If not, you become feeling-driven and do nothing, which eventually poisons your self-esteem.

When you fail at something because of poor preparation, you should feel ashamed, humiliated, and stupid— not for being dumb, but for not acting properly in preparing for the exam. The last thing you should do is attempt to protect your self-esteem. Everyone makes mistakes. But if you are committed to a master plan, you will take corrective action and thereby grow from your mistake. But if you try to make yourself feel good about a poor result in order to protect your self-esteem, you're stuffed.

You live in a society where too few people are real doers. It is important to understand, no matter how much your parents love you, or how committed your teachers are, you may be guided by people who have never attached themselves to a Master Dream List. Many people are not striving to live their wildest expectations. So rather than fail along the way, which every achiever does, they fail by not taking control of their lives. By not doing. They typically do only what feels comfortable.

THE GOLD COIN OF SELF-ESTEEM

Your self-esteem will be boosted in leaps and bounds doing the Mind Power exercises contained in this book. Listening to your affirmation tape is doing. Doing your goal-getting exercise is doing. Writing out your Master Dream List is doing. Defining the specific fixed daily activities is doing. Doing those fixed daily activities linked to your most immediate dream is doing.

But don't get me wrong. The paradox is you must like yourself. The Harvard Medical School once conducted a major study, which, of all things, determined that successful salespeople have certain basic psychological characteristics. The researchers wanted to know what traits were necessary to become successful at selling.

For our purposes, we are going to use selling as a metaphor for life. The one trait that was most dominant in successful salespeople was a strong, positive self-image. Basically these Ivy League researchers discovered that high achievers felt good about themselves, which means these people are doers. They felt good about themselves because they have always been in action towards a goal. Am I making sense? Action towards a goal boosts self-esteem.

Too many counselors, educators, and parents have this backwards. They would interpret this same research as proof that a person must feel good in order to succeed. Hey, this has become the standard approach to living. People are too concerned with feeling good and being comfortable. It sounds good, but nothing would ever get accomplished with this attitude. And Mary learns that she only has to do what she feels like doing. Ugh!

Boosting your self-esteem, which is the ultimate in feeling good, will only come on the heels of an accomplishment, or to a lesser degree as a result of doing the fixed daily activities leading to an accomplishment. Inactivity and non-linked action serve to lower self-esteem because there is no growth, no challenge, and no impending reward. All of which is common sense, I know.

But as Benjamin Franklin once said regarding common sense more than 200 years ago: "If it's so common, why is it so few people possess it?" You can say that again, Ben!

COMMON GROUND

Since you are in action, working from a master plan, it is important to make certain you continually program yourself positively. In other words, you are responsible for making yourself feel good. Don't rationalize failure, but find the common ground that will allow you to lick your wounds, pick yourself up, and get back in the game with confidence.

How do you feel about yourself? How do you feel when you are doing your fixed daily activities linked to your goal? Are you aware of when you feel good? Can you recognize it when you are feeling down? Do you know how to change how you feel by doing?

The bottom line is that you must be in touch with your feelings and know what to do about it when they are bad. Because most students and adults don't understand how to apply the powers of mind, they are hostage to their feelings. When they feel great, the sky's the limit; they're in a good mood and a joy to be around. But when they feel bad, get out of the way . . . get out of their way.

The real winners in life have a strong, positive self-image; they have confidence in their abilities and are far beyond the fear—be it fear of failure, fear of success, or fear of doing. Each goal that has been gotten builds confidence and boosts self-esteem, which is already on an elevated plane from doing the necessary fixed daily activities.

The common ground with all achievers is they consistently venture outside of their respective comfort zones working to get their goals. They have to feel uncomfortable in order to feel good about themselves. Got it? If it sounds like I'm talking a bunch of gibberish, relax and let's take a look at specific steps to building high self-esteem.

FIVE SELF-ESTEEM BOOSTERS

Self-esteem Booster Number 1: The Power of Perspective. You must learn the power of perspective. What that means is simple: You must learn to see things as they really are, not as you might imagine them to be. For instance, just because some teacher told you that you would never amount to anything does not mean you don't have a chance of being successful. Maybe there is a personality conflict between the two of you. Or possibly your teacher assumes your actions in his class are similar in everything you do.

Putting things in perspective is when you are able to recognize fact from fiction, aberration from the habitual, and that you are a capable person who is going achieve. If you have a bad coach, so be it. Putting things in perspective will allow you to continue improving as an athlete, and when you get a good coach, you'll be ready.

It is much easier to put things into perspective when you're working towards specific goals. First things first, do your fixed daily activities regardless of how you think or feel. The more mastery you have in Mind Power, the easier it is to recognize the negativity in the world, put it in perspective, and continue moving forward with an inner glow of enthusiasm.

Self-esteem Booster Number 2: The Positive Programming Cycle. Listen to your self-affirmation tape consistently. You continually will be bombarded with negative messages throughout your life. It is important that you learn how to redirect all the negativity around you, as well as your self-talk. As you know, you talk to yourself constantly and most self-statements people make are limiting, so you want to stay on top of this.

It's easy to get sidetracked in such a negative, media-driven, cynical world. Let's face it, people like to hear bad things about other people. Maybe it makes them feel better by being reminded that other people are worse off. Or it could be simply that misery loves company. Regardless, it's important to understand that most of your world will not be living in the positive programming cycle. You, your Dream Team Buddy, and a minority of enlightened achievers will—so you must always be on guard against the others.

I have dedicated all my adult life to the study of habits, mind power, and human potential. Let there be no mistake about it, the worst habit of all, the one that holds more people back from taking control over their lives than all other bad habits combined, is thinking. Most people have developed the self-limiting habit of living in the negative programming cycle. Many of your friends, if they aren't careful, are in the process of developing this life-ruining habit: focusing on negative thoughts, repeating negative thoughts, thinking of why something won't work out, etc. This becomes their self-fulfilling prophesy.

How often do you hear someone you know complaining about school? Lots, I'm sure. No matter what goals these people set for themselves, no matter how hard they appear to be working towards them, they will fail. Destructive Mind Power will never lead them to their dreams. Never.

Even though you have been working at controlling your programming cycle through the Mind Power exercises you already have been practicing, let's take a look at how well you are doing. Take out your Mind Power Notebook, get a clean page, write the date two days ago at the top and then write out every negative self-statement you can remember making over the past 48 hours. Come on, I know you still have negative thoughts. Nobody is completely free of them. The issue is being able to recognize the negative and consciously redirect them to the positive. Here is where you can use your control flame to support affirmation statements. After you complete this exercise, it is helpful to share it with your buddy if you have one. For example:

If you said:	Say instead:
"I hate French!"	"I love French!"
"She'll never go out with me."	"I am the best!"
"I don't like Ms. Smith."	"I communicate well with Ms. Smith."
"I'm afraid."	"I am full of confidence!"
"I'm stupid!"	"I'm smart and enjoy learning!"

You know the drill: recognize negative self-statements and completely turn them around. For most people, as simple as this appears in print, this is an awkward exercise. I know what some of you might be thinking—"You mean I have to tell myself 'I love French' when I hate it?"—many people have this train of thought at first. But most of you know the answer. Yes, of course you do—if you want to control your programming cycle.

Never be concerned with negative thoughts entering your mind. Don't be scared if doubt rears its ugly head. This is a natural occurrence that happens to everyone. You only set yourself up for failure when you expect to be free from these negatives because you've been listening to your affirmation tape, practicing your goal-getting exercise, or whatever. Your only concern need be to recognize and replace immediately with a positive counterpart.

Self-esteem Booster Number 3: Attack All Negative Self-beliefs. This is the action step for self-esteem booster number 2. Here you are taking action on your positive reprogramming statements. If you believe Ms. Smith doesn't think you are working hard enough in her class, you create an action plan that might influence Ms. Smith's opinion. Maybe you stay after class, volunteer for a special assignment, ask for personal assistance, sit in the front row, or increase your participation in class. Whatever you decide, it will always make you feel better about yourself to act in behalf of your reprogramming affirmation statements. You cannot control Ms. Smith's opinion, but you can certainly control how you respond.

If you feel unattractive, quit telling yourself how ugly you are and channel your energy into becoming the most attractive person you can be. Get some new clothes, change your hairstyle, take lessons in using makeup properly, imitate the look of some attractive movie star or model—the point is, do something. Guaranteed, you will feel better about yourself.

Self-esteem Booster Number 4: The Power of Positive Visualization. As you know, this is a consistent theme in constructive Mind Power. Visualization plays an important role in your goal-getting exercise, in living your wildest expectations, and it is also critical in building a healthy self-esteem. You must consistently create mental pictures of what it feels like to live your dreams.

I have already taken you through the paces of how to use this powerful technique. My intention is to make certain you realize how many ways you can apply it to your daily life. For example, you visualize how you're going to look in those new clothes, you see Ms. Smith calling on you in class, you develop the habit of changing your daydreams into goal-getting visualizations. This form of mental rehearsing, when accompanied with action, boosts self-esteem.

In a moment I am going to ask you to close your eyes, take a full breath, and visualize yourself living your most immediate dream from your goal-getting exercise, as if it were real now. See yourself full of confidence, feeling good about yourself in every way, just as you would like it to be. Okay, take a breath, close your eyes and visualize.

Not only should this be quite easy for you by now, it should be fun. As you continue to practice visualization within the structure of your goal-getting exercise, you are

conditioning your mind to form these images more naturally to where you can bring them up on call. When you
can control your daydreams in this manner, you have ar-
rived. And you will be consistently boosting your self-
esteem through visualization. Once again, this is doing.

Self-esteem Booster Number 5: The Power of Doing.
There is no way around the fact that action is linked to
your dreams. Everything comes back to your fixed daily
activities. In self-esteem booster number 3 you are acting
to counter negative self-belief. Here you are acting consistently with regard to getting your goal. The more discipline you apply to your daily routine, the better you feel,
the more you strengthen your self-esteem.

Whenever you feel down, after applying the other self-
esteem boosters, which shouldn't take but a few moments,
get involved in an appropriate fixed daily activity. It might
be exercise, studying, your goal-getting exercise, listening
to your affirmation tape, or contacting your buddy. The
issue is action. The more you do activities linked to your
dreams, the stronger your self-esteem. The less a person
acts, the lower his or her self-esteem. It's that simple.

SUMMARY AND SELF-TEST

Now you know. One of the critical components to constructive Mind Power is good healthy self-esteem. You've
gotta learn to like yourself in order to take control of your
life. Let's have a little fun and determine where you stand
by taking the following SEP—Self-Esteem Profile.

SEP: SELF-ESTEEM PROFILE

Instructions: This profile is designed to gauge your responses to various situations in life. The
objective is to help you become more

aware of how you really feel about yourself in various circumstances, and to avoid all those built-in defenses. For best results, answer each question honestly, as you are now. This will maximize your benefits from the exercise.

Upon reading each statement, circle the number under the answer which best describes you.

	Strongly Agree	Mildly Agree	Mildly Disagree	Strongly Disagree
1. I like myself.	4	3	2	1
2. I often question my abilities.	1	2	3	4
3. I think school would be easier if I had easier teachers.	1	2	3	4
4. I think about what could go wrong, rather than what could go right.	1	2	3	4
5. I often talk about my weaknesses.	1	2	3	4

6. I am easily intimidated by others.	1	2	3	4
7. I am easily influenced by peer pressure.	1	2	3	4
8. I am highly disciplined in doing my fixed daily activities.	4	3	2	1
9. I find myself distrustful of others.	1	2	3	4
10. Failure fuels my desire to work harder.	4	3	2	1

Scoring the Self-esteem Profile: You will determine your SEP score by adding all the numbers you have circled.

Maximum Score = 40   My Score _____

Score:

40–36   You're in great shape! Continue your Mind
         Power exercises and you will be living your
         wildest expectations.
35–29   Your self-esteem can use a little attention. It's
         close to being a powerful asset.
28–22   Average. Come on now, you can do better
         with a bit of work.

21–15   You better get busy strengthening your self-esteem. Reread this chapter and get commit yourself to all the Mind Power exercises.

14–10   Meet with your buddy and create an action plan directed at building your self-esteem immediately.

Regardless of how you scored, everyone has room for improvement. Review each question on the Profile and identify specific areas you need to work on. This is a good Dream Team Buddy exercise.

In the next chapter I'm going to introduce an activity that will compliment everything you do and go beyond simply boosting your self-esteem—it will activate the law of reciprocity: What goes around, comes around. At this stage, you're ready. First read this anonymous poem contrasting a winner and a loser. Think in terms of building self-esteem as you read it.

Winner vs. Loser

The Winner—is always part of the answer;

The Loser—is always part of the problem;

The Winner—always has a program;

The Loser—always has an excuse;

The Winner—says "Let me do it for you";

The Loser—says "That's not my job";

The Winner—sees an answer for every problem;

The Loser—sees a problem for every answer;

The Winner—sees a green near every sand trap;

The Loser—sees two or three sand traps near every green;

The Winner—says, "It may be difficult but it's possible";

The Loser—says, "It may be possible but it's too difficult."
Be a Winner!

WRAP-UP

- Action will help you feel good about yourself.
- High achievers have a strong, positive self-image.
- High achievers have developed that strong, positive self-image by setting and getting goals—doing.
- You are responsible for your self-esteem.
- Use the five Self-esteem Boosters.
- Mind Power exercises boost self-esteem.
- Be a doer!
- Be a winner!

Chapter 14

The Golden Rule of Successful Living

"The gifts that one receives for giving are so immeasurable that it is almost an injustice to accept them."

—Rod McKuen

One of the favorite exercises in my Mind Power workshops, for students and adults alike, is to ask everyone to read and explain Watty Piper's *The Little Engine That Could* to a child five years old or younger. If you have a younger brother, sister, nephew, or niece, read them this classic children's story one more time.

You know, "I think I can, I think I can, I think I can ...," said the little blue engine as it struggled to pull the train full of all kinds of presents for the boys and girls living on the other side of the mountain. Concluding with, "I thought I could, I thought I could, I thought I could ...," after the little blue engine had successfully climbed the hill and was chugging down the other side.

Not only was this little blue engine functioning in the positive programming cycle and controlling her self-talk, she was doing a good deed. As you might recall, the bigger engines refused to help the boys and girls on the other side of the mountain. The little blue engine was generous and acted accordingly. And through doing a good deed, boosted her self-esteem. Once again, action enters the self-esteem equation.

LIVING THE GOLDEN RULE

Most people have heard of the saying "What goes around, comes around." This is the law of reciprocity, and consider it one of those universal laws of nature. The problem is that few people actually act upon this law. Thinking about it, or believing in it, is one thing; doing something about it is another.

Hence the power of the Golden Rule: Treat other people how you would like to be treated. This might not make you appear "cool" under the scrutiny of negative peer pressure, but it will most definitely earn you respect. Think of when you saw a couple of bigger kids bully someone smaller, just to be mean. Or recall other more subtle acts such as ignoring a person at lunch, not including him in a pick-up basketball game, or teasing too hard. You probably see this happen many times every day. Why? Because it's human nature.

That's right. People have the tendency for both good and evil: to be mean-spirited or kind. Have we changed because of all the pressures of today's world? No. Sure, our toys have changed, but human nature remains a constant. Our mind still switches from constructive to destructive and back. This is why throughout all recorded history there has been some version of what has become known as "The Golden Rule" to help keep people away from evil and immersed in good. One of the simplest and most effective ways to improve relationships, all relationships, is to employ the Golden Rule in every aspect of life. Let's take a quick journey back in time with this law of nature. . . .

Confucius (551–479 B.C.):	"What you do not want done to yourself, do not do to others," from *The Chinese Classics* (1861–1886), volume 1, *The Confucian Analects*, translated by James Legge. This is the first recording of the Golden Rule.
Aristotle (384–322 B.C.):	"We should behave to our friends as we should wish our friends to behave to us," from *Lives of Eminent Philosophers*, book V, section 17, by Diogenes Laertius. This was recorded approximately 200 years after Confucius.
Matthew 7:12:	"Therefore all things ye would that men should do to you, do ye so to them: for this is the law of the prophets."

THE GOLDEN RULE AND MIND POWER

Is life really that simple? Yes and no. If you always treat other people as you would like to be treated, will they always reciprocate? No. There are plenty of fools in the world who would take advantage of their own grandmother if the opportunity presented itself. But, then again, these people are not working from a master plan. They are not in control of their lives.

Treat other people as you would like to be treated, and good things will come your way. Whether it's helping your mother with the dishes when you'd rather be on the phone with a friend, watching your neighbor's house while they are on vacation, or thinking of something nice to say every time you see the older lady who lives next door, kindness pays.

How? It's one of those conscious acts that makes you feel good. Think of the last time you did a favor for someone. How did you feel? The only way you would feel anything but great would be if you were taken advantage of—which is another story. My standard rule is to allow someone to take advantage of you one time, then put your foot down. Like the fools they are, there are those who will take advantage of you. Recognize them and avoid them thereafter.

How do you feel when an act of kindness is delivered your way? If it's genuine, with no strings attached, I'm certain you feel great. The point to understand concerns Mind Power. The more you apply the Golden Rule, the more natural it becomes to use your Mind Power constructively. Think of it like this: Good deeds help purge your system of life's poisons. No joke. This is exactly what happens.

Now let's take a closer look at the Golden Rule.

FOUR PARTS OF THE GOLDEN RULE

1. **Do Unto Others as You Would Want Them to Do Unto You.** This is the basic law of nature. It doesn't get much simpler, and it sets the tone for everything in life. You will always do well, wherever you go, by treating people as you would like to be treated.

2. **Think About Others the Way You Would Like Them to Think About You**. You know the power of thoughts. Good thoughts bring about good luck, which makes good things happen. Do you think bad thoughts about a certain teacher behind his back? If you do, stop it now. Not only is it destructive, it's the same negative energy that will hinder you from getting your goals.

3. **Empathize with People the Way You Would Like Them to Empathize with You**. The more you understand yourself, the easier it is to understand others. Sure, avoid negative people, but make certain you still send positive messages their way. They are not as enlightened as you, but someday they might see the light.

4. **Talk to Yourself the Way You Would Like Others to Talk to You**. This is the least understood aspect of the Golden Rule, and it's the foundation of Mind Power. How can you talk positively to someone, think good thoughts towards another, when you talk destructively to yourself? You can't. Sure, you can attempt to put on a good front, but the only person you're kidding is yourself. Be firm with how you talk to yourself.

DREAM TEAM BUDDY EXERCISE

Discuss a situation where you applied the Golden Rule, recall all the details. What prompted you? What specifically did you do? How was it received? How did you feel? Recall everything and discuss the situation as it relates to Mind Power and how it can be duplicated.

Now recall an incident where you weren't proud of yourself, where you missed the opportunity to apply the

Golden Rule, or, worse, where you acted with a mean spirit. Again, think of all the details. What prompted this action? What did you do? How was it received? How did you feel? Now relate how this impacted your use of Mind Power.

As you work through these reflections with your Dream Team Buddy, you become coach and coached, judge and judged, student and teacher, sinner and confessor. You need this sort of psychic cleansing to move forward in life. Nobody is perfect, and it's very helpful to be able to discuss life, warts and all.

The further you get into the philosophy of the Golden Rule, the more you will recognize the powerful role it can play throughout your journey of life. There will not always be immediate rewards, but rewards will always come your way in terms of developing the reputation of honesty, fairness, kindness, helpfulness, etc. All of us are only as good as our reputations.

THE POWER TO CONTROL

By understanding the basic laws of Mind Power, it's much easier for you to understand the value in terms of the programming power of the Golden Rule. Let's face it, you are what you think—right? It doesn't get any more basic: when you think good thoughts and do good deeds you are programming your subconscious mind for good things to happen in your life. You have activated that value antenna and it serves as a magnet for good happenings.

As enlightened people have understood for thousands of years, when you do favors for others, you receive direct benefits. It is always better to give than to receive. Think of the time you gave a present to someone you really cared about and relished in the joy the person expressed at your thoughtfulness. Contrast this with receiving a gift where, although you might enjoy the present, you feel a twinge of guilt being on the receiving end. I know this might be hard for some of you to swallow, but if you examine what I'm talking about closely it will make a lot of sense. There is no question about this issue and you will have the most significant impact on your life by applying it whenever you can.

When was the last time you felt you hated a classmate, teacher, brother, sister, or parent? Can you recall such a momentary transgression? Come on, everybody slips up on occasion. How did this impact your actions? How effective were you in doing what you needed to do? If I were to hazard a guess, your actions were not very constructive and you were not very effective at doing what you needed to do. When you fully understand the timeless principle of the Golden Rule, you know you can ill afford to hate or envy another human being. Why? Because it pulls you off-track from working towards your dreams.

My intention in sharing all of these Mind Power exercises is not only to help you achieve your goals but also to enable you to lead a more enjoyable life. You can let go of all of those slights you've been harboring in the back of your mind, give up on revenge or getting even, and focus on the old saying "Kill them with kindness."

Fire is doused with water, mean-spiritedness with goodness. Remember that the actions of others are outside your control and your job is to concern yourself only with what you can control. Living your life according to the Golden Rule is within your control. Let it become one of your main fixed daily activities. You will be rewarded accordingly.

Everyone loves tips, including students who are in the process of mastering Mind Power. So how about some tips? The next chapter is full of tips that can save you time and have an immediate impact. The tips concern studying and testing. Keep reading, I am certain you will find them very worthwhile.

WRAP-UP

- Read *The Little Engine That Could* to someone five years old or younger.
- Do a good deed every day. What goes around, comes around.
- Good deeds activate constructive Mind Power and build deep-seated confidence.
- Good deeds are a DO.
- The Golden Rule is timeless: remember Confucius, Aristotle, and Matthew.
- Apply all four parts of the Golden Rule:

  1. Do unto others as you would want them to do unto you.
  2. Think about others as you would want them thinking about you.
  3. Empathize with others the way you would want them to feel about you.
  4. Talk to yourself the way you would want others to talk to you.

Chapter 15

Mind Power Studying and Testing Tips

"The secret of education lies in respecting the pupil."

— Ralph Waldo Emerson

Like anything else, learning is a skill that can be taught. The best teachers naturally cover this topic, but, alas, there is not enough time or attention devoted to this skill to make certain everyone gains mastery of the learning process. Too much emphasis is placed on knowledge that can be accessed on-line rather than how to make learning a lifelong habit.

It may have been a long time since a teacher went into any great detail as to the basics of how to take notes in class, do homework, study for tests, and take tests. Before you start getting aggravated with your teachers, please understand they are merely pawns of the system, a system that would rather count the percentages of students that pass from grade to grade than take the time to determine how many are actually learning.

You, my friend in Mind Power, are about to learn the tricks of the trade. Apply them with what you have already learned and you will have discovered the shortcut to time-efficient, high-powered learning.

SEVEN BASIC PRINCIPLES OF LEARNING

1. **Step-by-Step**: Forget about cramming for your exams. Sure, you might be able to memorize enough material to pass, but what a waste of time—your ability to retain what you've supposedly learned is horrible! Learning is designed to be one step at a time. You didn't learn how to walk with your first step, talk with your first words, or ride a bike on your first attempt. Classroom learning is no different. For that matter, neither is on-the-job skill training.

   Learn to pace your learning. Do your assignments as you receive them. Homework should be completed nightly. If you have a project that is due in three weeks, work on it a little bit every day until you get most of it completed. Effective learning requires moderation: neither too fast nor too slow, but steady as you go.

2. **Constant Repetition:** This is no different than performing your goal-getting exercise every day. The more something is repeated, the more it sinks in. The more you rewrite your Master Dream List, the more committed you will become to your dreams. The more a third-grader rewrites and recites the spelling of Mississippi, the more that youngster is likely to learn how to spell it.

3. **Ongoing Support**: Because learning is constantly forcing you outside of your comfort zone, it is essential that you have a support system to lean on. Your Dream Team Buddy will naturally provide such support. Parents who understand

the rules of Mind Power can also serve this purpose, but be careful of parents who hinder learning by creating pressure.

Your Dream Team Buddy is not only going to
support you but will also hold you accountable
for doing the necessary activities associated with
learning: homework, studying, library time, etc.
And, yes, your buddy will give you ongoing
feedback as to how you are coming along.

4. **Doing and Teaching**: You must actively apply
what you know in order to fully learn—whether
it's going over your lessons with a family member, your buddy, or simply teaching yourself
through application. I am currently doing both,
as this chapter is being written on a word-
processing software system that is new to me.
Not only am I using it, doing, I'm going to teach
this system to my wife—which will reinforce
what I have already learned.

5. **Controlling Your Environment**: I have seen
students attempt to complete their homework at
the kitchen table while everyone else was finishing dinner. Others make a habit of reading their
assignments while falling asleep in bed. Some
listen to rock music, others watch television, and
on and on. You probably know someone who
does one, if not all, of the above. No good!

When you want to listen to rock 'n 'roll, take
a break and listen. If there is a television program you want to watch, watch it and enjoy.
When you are ready for sleep, get in bed and
crash. All this is common sense, I know. But
when you are ready to do your homework or
study, it's very helpful to have a work station
just for that activity.

There are different schools of thought on this subject. What I have found that works best is to find an area that has good lighting, is relatively quiet, and has ample room for your materials. This area can be in your bedroom, dining room, den, cellar, tree-fort—it doesn't really matter. What is important is that you are able to concentrate and have minimal interruptions, and you can associate that location with learning.

6. **Time Blocking**: The fact is that most people can apply maximum concentration for about 20 minutes at one sitting. So, does this mean you need only study for 20 minutes? Yes and no. No, you are going to need far more than 20 minutes to be a lifelong learner. Yes, you should take mini-breaks about every 20 minutes; get something to drink, walk the dog, make a five-minute phone call, talk sports with your buddy, etc. Then get right back into your work for another 20 minutes.

7. **Control Flame**: No matter how well you block your time, nor how effective your study environment, your mind will wander. Typically this creates frustration. Not for you. Before you begin your learning session, you are to simply visualize your control flame, take a belly breath, and affirm, "I have total concentration and absorb knowledge." Then begin your studies. Whenever your mind wanders while studying or doing homework, use your control flame as if you were starting over and guide your concentration back to the task at hand.

You will also use your control flame before and during every quiz and test. I will get into more detail on this later. Winston Churchill had an interesting concept regarding learning and it's worth keeping in the back of your mind: "I am always ready to learn, but I do not always like being taught." Think in terms of teaching yourself as you apply the tips outlined in this chapter.

READING TO LEARN

This might appear sacrilegious at first glance, but bear with me. Whenever you have a reading assignment—let's say you have to read Chapter 10 for class discussion tomorrow—the following steps will prove very helpful.

1. First, begin with the summary at the back of the chapter. This will give you an idea of what the author was attempting to convey in the chapter.
2. Next, read and attempt to answer the questions at the end of the chapter. Much like reading the summary, you are getting a flavor of what the author wants you to learn. This is also what most teachers want you to learn.
3. Now you are ready to skim the chapter by only reading the headings, bold print, underlined phrases, and picture or graph captions.
4. Read the chapter. If you are thinking to yourself, "Hey, I won't need to read the chapter now," you're almost right, but not quite. You must still read the chapter.
5. Answer all the questions at the end of the chapter. You must not leave this chapter until you can answer all the questions. If you have difficulty with any, go back through the chapter, isolate the necessary subject matter, reread it, and study it until you can answer the questions.

The difference in learning will be incredible. This is why you want to get into the habit of going step by step;

it will always save you time in the long run. Most students want to rush through their assignments, read through the chapter as fast as possible, and thus learn very little.

Once again, answer the questions at the end of the chapter, but this time write out your answers. If you can not answer all the questions, review the headlines within the chapter until you find the information you need to learn, reread it, and learn it. Do not leave the chapter until you know what they author wanted you to know.

READING, NOTES, AND STUDYING

If you want to cut your study time back even more, take notes while you read your assignments. I know this might appear tedious, but it will definitely accelerate your retention, and lessen the time you will need preparing for a test.

You will begin your note taking when you commence your actual reading of the chapter. Actually, it's a simple process that I discovered from Dr. Falkenberg, a professor of psychology at Wake Forest University in Winston-Salem, North Carolina. Dr. Falkenberg has created a learn-to-learn course that includes what he terms the "readrite" system. It consists of three basic steps: looking over the material, taking notes, and self-testing. The preparation for reading the chapter will suffice as looking it over; self-testing is answering the questions before and after; but, with regard to note taking, Dr. Falkenberg has a unique twist.

He wants you to begin reading, and read as much as you can recall at one time, whether it's a paragraph, a page, or a chart. Then you are to write a sentence or two that summarizes what you have just read. The idea is to write your notes from memory, not to reread in order to take notes. Once you have completed your first readrite section, begin the process again. I think this is brilliant!

His theme with this exercise is to read-remember-write. Makes good sense, doesn't it? Or can you remember what you have just read?

TESTING TIPS

No matter how well you learn, you must learn how to do well on tests. Too many students choke on exams. I don't know why. All anyone ever tells you is that you better get an A or you will spend the rest of your life cleaning toilets for a living. Pressure? Nah! Most fifth-graders can not comprehend a life cleaning toilets. But most high school and college students do feel the pressure, subtle or blatant, to excel. And test time is game time.

So here's the drill. Relax. Use your control flame to continually purge your system of worry, anxiety, fear, and whatever negative emotions you might associate with testing. You must also use your flame during the exam, from the moment you enter the room, place your name on the test, and begin answering questions. Whenever you feel that surge of anxiety, flame it.

The control flame will guarantee that your subconscious mind will participate in this learning challenge. Your testing affirmation should be something like, ''I am relaxed and have total memory recall,'' or maybe simply, ''I have total memory recall.''

Before you begin answering the test questions, make certain you know how the test is to be scored. Are you being graded on the number of correct answers versus the number of questions? If so, you had better finish the entire exam and leave no blanks. Or are you being graded on the percentage of correct responses of the questions you have answered? This isn't usually the case, but whenever it is, you should eliminate obviously incorrect answers and then make your best guess. The best rule of thumb is to determine whether you are expected to complete the exam. Some tests are intentionally designed not to be completed. For the sake of both simplicity and the law of averages, I am going to assume you are being graded on the number you get correct versus the number of questions on the test. The following guidelines will work wonders:

- Read each question slowly, carefully, and in a relaxed manner.
- Answer all questions that you can easily answer.
- Place a √ mark next to any question you are unsure of the answer.
- After answering all the easy questions, return to your √ marked questions.
- Visualize your control flame, affirm "I have total memory recall," read the question, and write down the first thought that comes into your mind.

You will be amazed at how your mind will work for you using this format. Let me explain. Whenever you get stuck on a question, let's say it's question 7, and wrack your brain to try to get an answer, you create frustration which actually serves to hinder your natural ability to recall. In other words, it messes you up for the rest of the test. Ugh!

But by simply skipping those difficult questions, marking them with a √, and continuing reading and answering the questions you are certain about, you are activating your ability to recall. It's almost as though you are warming it up. You are also triggering various memories by slowly reading and answering the questions you are confident about. By the time you return to these questions, use your control flame and reread the question—the odds are that you will know the answer. Somehow, someway, your subconscious mind will pull you through.

All it will take is one test to develop complete confidence in this testing process. I have watched students who were once petrified of tests, choked regularly and often failed, gain a feeling of control, which boosted confidence, and the test scores improved so dramatically some were actually accused of cheating. In one sense they were. They were cheating by understanding the game of studying, learning, and testing. Let's face it, it's a game, and you might as well learn how to play it—and then play to win.

VISUALIZATION

You will find it extremely helpful to spend a few moments visualizing both your study sessions and your test taking. Every day you practice your goal-getting exercise and visualize your goals and fixed daily activities, make certain to picture yourself either doing your homework or studying. Whenever a test looms on the horizon, you will want to see yourself taking that particular exam. The following are a few pointers.

Studying/ Homework: Picture yourself in your selected study spot where you have controlled the environment. Visualize yourself having total concentration, using your control flame to strengthen your concentration, and picture yourself literally absorbing knowledge. See yourself actually enjoying the learning process, learning effectively and rapidly—just as you would like it to be.

Testing: You will want to see yourself getting up in the morning full of confidence, arriving at school relaxed, confident, and looking forward to the challenge of testing your knowl-

edge. Visualize using your control
flame, see yourself entering the
classroom, getting your test paper,
using your flame again, affirming "I
am relaxed with total memory recall," and then see yourself answering all the questions with total
memory recall—enjoying the challenge of testing. See yourself finishing and getting the grade you want.

Whether you are taking the SATs, the LSATs, the bar
exam, or a spelling quiz, the fundamentals remain the
same. The better prepared you are in learning, the more
knowledge you have acquired. The more relaxed and in
control of the testing process you are, the easier it is for
you to showcase your knowledge. Your control flame
will give you a tremendous advantage, both in studying
and when testing. It is amazing when you think about it
that one tool will strengthen concentration and facilitate
the absorption of information, and at a later date allow
you to relax and experience total memory recall. What a
deal!

ADDITIONAL THOUGHTS . . .

When establishing your fixed daily activities with your
Dream Team Buddy, make certain to be very time specific
about your homework and studying. You want it to be a
routine: same time, same place, same process, same
amount of time. Naturally, there will be variations, but for
the most part you want a standardized routine. Whether
you study with your buddy on Tuesdays and Thursdays

in the library after school, or only get together once a week, be consistent.

WRAP-UP

- Make learning into a process.
- Follow the Seven Basic Learning Principles: step-by-step, constant repetition, ongoing support, doing and teaching, controlling your environment, time blocking, and control flame.
- Reread the five Steps for reading to learn.
- Understand Dr. Falkenberg's readrite system: look it over, take notes, test yourself.
- Your control flame will help tremendously in both studying and testing.
- Visualize yourself studying and testing—just as you would like it to be.

Chapter 16

Mind Power and Sports

"Great athletes acknowledge that 60 to 90 percent of success in sports is due to mental factors."
—Psychologist Charles Garfield

Dr. Gabe Mirkin, author of *The Sportsmedicine Book* (Boston, Little, Brown, 1978), once asked more than 100 top-level runners the simple question, "If I could give you a pill that would make you an Olympic champion—and also kill you in a year, would you take it?" More than half said Yes!

Not that you are a competitive runner, or necessarily want to die in a year, but the fact is that people place tremendous importance upon how they perform on the athletic field. I watch golf enthusiasts spend a small fortune on the latest clubs, lessons, and green fees—only to let their mind function destructively every time they play a round of golf. Just a fraction of the Mind Power techniques you already understand would help most any athlete gain that elusive competitive edge.

This book is not the vehicle to get into great detail on specific mind game strategies for individual sports. Each sport has its own nuances that require special attention. But constructive Mind Power is a commonality within all successful athletes. I can recall clearly when my high school wrestling career hit rock-bottom. I choked in a tournament that I was seeded to win. By allowing my mind to run off destructively, I got pinned in the second round of the tournament. Talk about being embarrassed! Even at the ripe old age of sixteen I was able to recognize that my mind caused the problem. That flash of insight was only in hindsight—but what a lesson learned!

MIND POWER RULES

Whether you are an archer, field goal kicker, golfer, tennis player, basketball junkie, sandlot baseball player—once the fundamentals of any sport are learned, the rest of it is a mind game. Any active athlete or coach will quickly confirm this. But intellectual understanding and practical application are not one and the same.

Whenever you read an article on sports, if you have your Mind Power antenna up, it's very likely you will recognize some inference to the mind. It just happened to me as I picked up the sports section of *USA Today* in a break from my final—hopefully—edit of this chapter. It was the September 15, 1995, issue and the feature sports story was about Don Baylor, the manager of baseball's Colorado Rockies. Brent Saberhagen, an All-Star pitcher who has played for eight managers and currently plays for Baylor, described Baylor's effective management style—his words offer insight into the difference between understanding and application. "It's refreshing," Saberhagen said. "After a while you keep hearing. 'You guys stink' and 'You guys are playing stupid,' and you start to believe it. Don's the only guy I've seen come in after a tough loss and say, 'Keep on battling. We're still in this thing.'"

How's that for recognizing Mind Power? Now for my point. . . .

The other professional managers and coaches Saberhagen has encountered throughout his baseball career may have understood the importance of Mind Power, but obviously, with the exception of Don Baylor, none were able to put it into application. Either they never developed the habits or lacked the practical tools for application. Regardless. . . .

This is an indictment on how seldom Mind Power tools are actually being applied. No wonder students are not exposed to the fundamentals in school when many professional athletic coaches and managers, who may understand these fundamentals, fail to apply them. And it's so simple! You already know the three fundamentals, let me refresh you in the context of sports.

THREE MIND POWER FUNDAMENTALS

All you need to remember is your self-talk/affirmations, your control flame, and visualization. You will use your control flame to flush any negative thoughts, feelings or emotions—much the same as you would relative to a test. If you feel yourself getting nervous about the game that evening, use your flame to purge that negative programming. Your affirmation will depend on your sport, but it should center around relaxation, confidence, concentration, smooth movement, and winning. You will visualize during your suggestive relaxation exercise, seeing yourself playing just as you would want to play, and in the midst of performing. A tennis player pictures exactly where his serve is going, the golfer visualizes his stroke, the baseball player can see himself hitting the baseball while in the on-deck circle, the gymnast visualizes her routine in the locker room, and so on.

PUTTING IT ALL TOGETHER

A tennis player might use the control flame after hitting a bad shot to center her emotions and affirm to herself, "I move my feet, meet the ball early, and win." A baseball player might use the control flame in the on-deck circle, awaiting his chance to hit, to relax and center while affirming, "I see the ball clearly and make good contact." A golfer should use the control flame following a pre-shot visualization routine before every stroke. The idea is to lock in the visual image of where the ball is going to land, center the mind and body, and affirm something like, "Head down, slow back swing, and natural power."

None of this is very difficult. The more relaxed you are under the competitive pressures on the playing field, the more of an advantage you have, just as with memory recall during a test. Choking is choking; it's no different in the classroom than it is on the playing field. Your role, as an athlete, is to make certain your mind is working constructively. You want it to help you, not hurt you. The more you can talk to yourself properly during the heat of the competition, the more the advantage is yours. I have seen inferior athletes defeat athletes possessing far superior physical skills simply by using their minds.

How often to you hear an athlete talk to his or herself about exactly what they don't want to do? It happens all the time, "I always miss that shot!" "I stink!" "I can't make a putt!" and the self-defeating talk athletes have with themselves goes on and on. I love hearing this from my opponent on the tennis court. It signals a glaring weakness, and unless this person is a significantly superior tennis player, I am going to kick butt! One of my tennis friends, a federal prosecutor who is used to hearing criminals talk trash, can't break himself of the habit of talking trash to himself on the court. He can be three courts away, but whenever anyone hears the scream, "You Twinkee!" we know Bobby's game is in trouble. On the other hand, positive statements indicate an athlete is in control. The following are examples of basic self-talk statements that are frequently used while playing.

- Watch the ball.
- Head down.
- All net.
- Move your feet.
- Be aggressive.
- Win!
- Smooth swing.
- Hands up.

Get the idea? Visualization is also essential in sports. You can elevate your game to the next level by devoting five to ten minutes every day simply visualizing yourself playing exactly as you would like to play. Like every other aspect of *Mind Power for Students*, it's a discipline, a mental discipline. Too many athletes don't have time for the mental side and their game suffers as a result.

Your visualization should include as much sensory detail as possible. Not only do you want to picture yourself playing, you want to sense every aspect of your sport. Whether it's hitting a baseball, dunking a basketball, or swimming your heats, the more sensory-alive your images, the more impact they will have on your performance.

There you have it. And I guarantee that if you apply these three basic fundamentals to your athletic career, you will be more advanced than many professional athletes— advanced in Mind Power, that is.

WRAP-UP

- Mind Power techniques will provide an edge in any sport.
- There are three fundamentals: self-talk/affirmations, control flame, and visualization.
- Your control flame will keep you centered and free of negative tension.

- Your affirmation self-talk will allow you to stay in control under pressure, and, most important, avoid self-defeating talk.
- Visualization is essential to Mind Power in sports: see yourself playing exactly as you would like to play.
- Use your common sense, as similarities abound between testing and sports.

Chapter 17

Just Do It!

"As I grow older, I pay less attention to what people say. I just watch what they do."
—Andrew Carnegie

Mind Power is not an intellectual endeavor. It's not something you just read about, think about, discuss with a friend, and then sleep on it. Mind Power requires action. You have been exposed to a lot since beginning this journey into Mind Power; yet the benefits, those positive results, will only happen as a result of you taking action. No matter what your vantage point, you can not get away from doing if you want any changes in your life.

Take the chapter on the Golden Rule, for example. It's unlikely you learned anything new about this timeless rule, except possibly from a more historical perspective. But from a practical viewpoint, everyone knows they should treat others as they would like to be treated themselves. Whenever I ask an audience if they believe in the saying, "What goes around, comes around," the response is always 100 percent yes. Heck, the Golden Rule is basically 4,000 years old!

But knowledge itself is not power, rather it's application of knowledge that is powerful. Knowing about something and doing something about it are often as different as night and day. In order to live up to your wildest expectations, you have committed your life to that of a doer.

I have listened to students, athletes, and adults speak

so earnestly about what they want to do: make the team ... get into law school ... get a promotion at work ... but they never seem to change what they are doing. I don't see them taking extra practice, sacrificing social life for a structured study schedule, or working overtime to earn that promotion. It seems that there is always some excuse and they are continually getting ready to get ready to begin tomorrow. They develop a habit of rationalizing their inactivity.

You, or anyone actively involved with this book and the exercises contained therein, are acting towards your Master Dream List.

I find myself continually paraphrasing an old saying—it sums up this issue quite well: "Your actions speak so loudly I can't hear what you say." Too many people fall into the trap of talking a good game—great, if you can back it up with action—but most big talkers are small on doing. They talk instead of act. Your challenge is to act on the exercises in this book when you don't have all the confidence you might like, when you don't quite believe in yourself or your abilities. It's okay to be unsure at times, but always remember that using your mind constructively, taking control of your life, working from a master plan, living your wildest expectations—all require action.

Think back to your role models, the achievers you know. Are they doers? Most likely they are. Did they always have confidence and believe in themselves? No. Many were searching for meaning in their lives, for answers, and working toward dreams while still having doubts. But the fact is they acted. They acted in the face of their fears, doubts, questions, and challenges. Through action they were able to strengthen their confidence and build belief in themselves and their abilities. And naturally through such action, their abilities increased.

Nearly 100 years ago, the founding father of psychology in America, Professor William James, reflected about his thoughts on action: "Seize the very first possible opportunity to act on every resolution, and every emotional prompting you experience in the direction of the habits you aspire to gain." That makes as much sense today as it did when the great Harvard professor was in his prime. How are you doing in terms of action? Have you jumped into these Mind Power exercises, seized the opportunity, and begun to take control of your life?

YOUR ACCOUNTABILITY TEST

Take out your Mind Power Notebook, get a blank page and write today's date and "Accountability" at the top. Do you have a Mind Power Notebook? Some of these Do's are very elementary. You have been exposed to many pearls of wisdom throughout these chapters, but, as you know, they mean nothing if they are not acted upon. You wouldn't be pleased with my Mind Power coaching if I failed to hold you accountable for doing what you are learning.

Thus I am going to be firm with you. Draw a line down the middle of the page. On the top-right side of the page, write your Dream Team Buddy's name. You do have a buddy, don't you?! On the top-left side, write your name. Under each of your names, write in bold print "My Five Do's" and then numerically list 1 through 5. Here I want you to each to list five exercises you have put into action thus far. Be it making a self-affirmation tape, using the control flame, the studying tips, connecting with a Dream Team Buddy, list five areas where you have been proactive. When you have finished listing what you have done, again in bold print write "My Five To-Do's" and number 1 through 5 beneath the heading. Now it's time to determine what you need to act upon—NOW!

For example, if you have made your affirmation tape, you write that as one of your five Do's. If you have completed your Master Dream List, that's a Do. If you have yet to use your control flame, or do your goal-getting exercise, this is a To-Do.

This is a great Dream Team Buddy exercise, as you can review each other's lists and determine which To-Do's need doing immediately. You should go through this exercise each time you get one of your goals, as you need to adjust your goals at this point. Getting your goals and, living your dreams will always require breaking them down into fixed daily activities. This is the lowest component part of any goal or dream—the daily Do's. Without them, nothing worthwhile will ever happen.

MASTERING THE ACHIEVEMENT CYCLE

Once you have grasped the basics of Mind Power, nothing is more important than mastering the Cycle of Achievement you learned about in Chapter 11. Forget about how you feel or think and simply do what is necessary to achieve your desired result. Mastery of this cycle will provide a lifetime habit that will do more than have you continually getting your goals: you will be continually building your confidence and self-esteem to such levels that nothing—nothing—will be able to interfere with your maintaining absolute control over your life.

You will be tempted to fall into destructive patterns. Be alert to this, but recognize that it's only normal. Most people are feeling driven and want people to share similar feelings. Whether it's anger, apathy, cynicism, or a host of other negative emotions, your job is to be able to quickly recognize destructive Mind Power and act accordingly.

Does this mean you can't have fun? Heck, no! I want you to have a blast. Go to the games, dances, parties . . . participate in sports, drama club, school politics . . . but always adhere to the rules of constructive Mind Power.

Avoid negative people. Make your decisions according to the Golden Rule. Always make certain you have completed your fixed daily activities and are able to perform them tomorrow as well. In other words, there is a distinct difference between having fun and being stupid. Messing with drugs or getting dead drunk is stupid, having fun at a party is fun. Drugs and booze can ruin your life, much less get you off track from getting your goals. Attending a party is a healthy release.

Let's take another look at the inner workings of the Cycle of Achievement:

Goal (dream)–Doing–Thinking–Feeling–Goal (dream)

This is your foundation for every good habit in your life. Repetition of an act makes a habit, repetition of an act that is linked to a goal or dream creates the magical habit of achievement and allows you to discover a wonderful law of nature—the Law of Control.

Now let's briefly revisit each component of this Cycle of Achievement and relate it to where you are now and the progress you've already made:

Goal: Establishing real goals is an activity. It is a Do. Without breaking your Master Dream List into short-term, time-specific goals, your activity might take the form of the proverbial dog chasing its tail. You could easily find yourself spinning your wheels and going nowhere. So, are you comfortable with your goal-getting exercise? Have you thought through the specific targets, time parameters, etc.? This is like your beginner's road map. You can't begin your journey without it.

Doing: Creating your goals, reading this book, breaking your goals down into fixed daily activities, doing your fixed daily activities—are all Do's. These are activities which require your controlled involvement—DOING. Like creating your goals and fixed daily activities, you are completely in control over this component. This is the action phase of the Cycle of Achievement because it dictates the remaining components. Whenever you're feeling lazy, remember, action cures fear, action builds confidence, action strengthens self-esteem, and action gets goals.

To master the powers of your mind and live your dreams, you have to become a doer. You need to consistently act, often upon something you might not feel favorable about. You might want to watch Monday night football instead of doing your scheduled schoolwork. Sorry, do your work first and then watch some of the game. I'd rather be watching Sunday night baseball on ESPN, but not until I finish this chapter—I'll catch the tail end and the highlights. So be it. That's the life of an achiever.

Also, there will be times when you have to act upon something that is unpleasant to you. Maybe it's homework in a particular subject you dislike, exercising to get in shape, or helping out around the house. Here doing might create tension, but so does committing to goals. Work through the tension, it comes with the turf.

Thinking: You know my thinking about thinking. How's that for a play on words? We all have voluntary and involuntary thoughts. By now you realize that most people think far too much and are therefore locked into that negative programming cycle. They have developed the habit of self-limiting thinking,

dwelling on negatives until they turn
into worries which sabotage the best of
intentions. Worry is a mental cancer; it
will slowly eat away at your dreams
and create a life of quiet desperation.

But, not to worry. You are a doer. Action cures fear
and will help keep you free of this mental cancer. There
is one obstacle. The easiest course of action for most people trapped in the negative programming cycle is to act
according to their existing programming. This means to
do nothing. Ouch! Acting against negative thoughts will
force you outside your comfort zone, which is exactly
where you want to live your life. Don't expect to live
your dreams staying in your comfort zone.

Many of your Mind Power exercises will impact your
thinking. Listening to your affirmation tape, doing your
goal-getting exercise, spending time with your Dream
Team Buddy . . . all will have a positive impact on how
you think. Just remember, it's not what you think, it's
what you do.

Feeling: When was the last time you felt like doing your homework? Or how about the
last time you got really mad? Human beings have a wide range of feelings. They
are as much a part of what make us
unique as our ability to do and think. Joy,
excitement, fear, anger, nervousness,
love, laziness, pride, and on and on they
go. How do most people, not just students, act? They act in accordance with
how they feel. If it feels good, they do
it.

This seems to be universal. People only consistently do
what feels comfortable. When was the last time you heard

someone moan, ''Ah, man, I just didn't feel like it''? The odds are they were referring to something they didn't do, and how they felt was their excuse. Lame! But you hear it every day. It's the path of least resistance, and let me assure you, most people are deep down that path—and it's a path to nowhere, for they have no options.

YOUR OPTIONS

Your life is full of options. The more you apply the Cycle of Achievement goal–doing–thinking–feeling–goal to the Mind Power techniques in this book, the more control you will have over every aspect of your life.

Your job is to stay in motion and live your wildest expectations, continually reset and get your goals, and begin checking off your accomplished dreams, one at a time, from your Master Dream List. Get used to being uncomfortable, reread this book, review the notes in your Mind Power Notebook, and Act Now!

Activity will always drive the dream, control your thoughts, impact your feelings, and get you those goals. Or as Nike tells the world, JUST DO IT!

POSTSCRIPT

Once you have made a habit of using your mind constructively, when you have mastered the tools I have shared with you, share this book with your parents. If that's not possible—or, in some cases, not advisable—share it with some adult who you respect. Make certain they read it and perform the exercises. Not only will you be sharing your gift, you will be playing a bit of role reversal. You, my soul mate in Mind Power, will become the teacher. How's that for a simple twist of fate.

I'd wish you luck, but you will be making your own

· luck. This is not the end, it's just the beginning, so have
a wonderful journey through life. And, at all times, remember, you are in control, through Mind Power. Cheers!

WRAP-UP

- How are you doing?
- Remember, your actions will always speak louder
  than your words.
- Think of your five Do's.
- Commit to your five To-Do's.
- The Cycle of Achievement is the foundation of all
  good habits.
- Achievers are doers.
- Most people are feeling driven, neither doers nor
  achievers.
- Just do it!
- Share this book with an adult you respect.
- Assume the role of Mind Power teacher to this
  adult.
- Enjoy your journey!